Love Letters *from* Heartbreak Ridge

Love Letters *from* Heartbreak Ridge

Kathy Poulsen Romero

HAPPY DAY
PUBLISHING

Love Letters from Heartbreak Ridge
Copyright © 2024 by Kathy Poulsen Romero
All rights reserved, including the right to reproduce
distribute, or transmit in any form or by any means.

Except as permitted under the U.S. Copyright Act of 1976, no part of this book may be reproduced, distributed, or transmitted in any form or by any means, or stored in a database or retrieval system without the written permission of the authors, except in the case of brief passages embodied in critical reviews and articles where the title, author and ISBN accompany such review or article.

For information contact:

kathypromero@gmail.com

authorkathyromero.com

Published by:

Happy Day Publishing

Cover design and interior book design by
Francine Platt, Eden Graphics, Inc.

Paperback ISBN 979-8-89454-017-7

eBook ISBN 979-8-89454-018-4

Library of Congress Number: 2024915722

Manufactured in the United States of America

Dedicated to my dear brother, Todd ~
who completed our family.

To my husband Mike ~
my partner, soulmate and best friend.

To my daughter Eliza ~
for all your countless hours of help that
kept me going.

And, to our entire military ~
past, present and future.

"Our debt to the heroic men and valiant women in the service of our country can never be repaid. They have earned our undying gratitude."

– HARRY S. TRUMAN

Dear Lila,

I received your last ve[tter] the other day and was [ ] eased to hear from you again. [ ] said, the letter's mean a gre[at deal to] a person when your so far aw[ay from home]. I really do appreciate your [letters to] me Lila, as your letter's hel[p a] great deal in cheering me up.

From the way I talked I [guess you] really got a horrible impres[sion of the] Army. I may have exaggerated [a bit] at, but all in all the Army [isn't] it any good as far as I'm c[oncerned.] guess I am just too much of a [home bod]y, as I always have been. It [isn't so] much the being away from [home th]at bothers me, but also the [way we] are treated by our so-cal[led su]periors. No kidding, Lila, we ar[e treated] just like so much dirt under [foo]t. I didn't think I would ever ha[ve to ta]ke off anyone what I've had [to tak]e, but there isn't much [to be] done about it, so I may as [well ma]ke the best of it. Like so man[y]

FOREWORD

For more than seventy years, a tattered box lay hidden in the old home's downstairs closet, untouched and unknown to anyone but the long-deceased owner of that box–my mother.

As I carefully untied the yellowed, brittle lace ribbon that secured the box, then lifted its lid, I discovered not just a few, but a trove of letters carefully preserved, as if waiting patiently for me to find them and liberate the inner most feelings of a young soldier going off to fight in the Korean War. More than its historic value and firsthand documentation of events that are today taught in history books, these letters were, to me, of greater personal value–documenting my parents' courtship and giving me much needed insight into the heart and mind of a man I never really knew–my father.

The old box contained every letter and card that my parents had sent each other, beginning with my mom's first letter to then Pvt. Medford Poulsen to the final penned elation, "I'm coming home!"

Hunting down an aged family photo album that I remembered seeing as a child, I found the pictures that had been contained with the letters and corroborated the geographical landscape and passage of time the letters traversed. I was able to put the actual photographs with the letters and envelopes they'd been entrusted with.

My dad records his experiences in a way that his full range of emotions are shared through his growing love for his Lila, as well as the horrors of war and his deepest fears of serving in a foreign battle he didn't know if he would ever return from.

I share these letters exactly as they were written. Some are love letters, others give a graphic account of historic events that he witnessed. Perhaps none were more evocative than his time spent at Korea's infamous Heartbreak Ridge, where he was assigned to the prestigious, and bloody, 7th Infantry Division.

Times were different then, as you will see in how women were talked to. There are some expressions used that were indicative of the frustrations of war. It was a different time, and yet the emotions, fears and, most of all, the young couple's yearning love, can still be understood and felt today.

Here was my father, cold and aloof to me in the flesh, yet now sharing with me his most intimate feelings.

This story does not end with my father's final letter. I hope you will be as profoundly affected by the letters as I was, all the way to the final chapter–a journey which took me decades and a lifetime to finally understand.

How are you doing way down [in] Texas? I guess you probably [like it better] there than you did in Kansas [?]

I think Jerry told you she [gave me] your address. She said she was [going] to. I'm not too good at writ[ing letters] but I'll try. Because I [ap]preciate letters from anyone even [a little] blonde girl that Jerry told [me about]. (I read one of your letters - do you [know what] you I'll do.

It sure would be nice if [you and] Doug happened to by chance [be stationed] in the same camp.

Jerry sure does miss him. She [does]n't know what to do half of [the time].

CHAPTER ONE

The Opening Letters

"But, due to the way we are treated
I sometimes wonder if we have any
           more rights than the prisoners do
and that's no kidding."

Feb 18, 1951

Hi Med,

How are you doing way down there in Texas? I guess you probably like it better there than you did in Kansas, don't you?

I think Gerrie told you she gave me your address? She said she was going to. I'm not too good at writing letters but I'll try because if you appreciate letters from anyone, even that tall blonde girl Gerrie told you about (I read one of your letters — do you mind?), maybe I'll do.

It sure would be nice if you and Doug happened to by chance get placed in the same camp. Gerrie sure does miss him. She doesn't know what to do half of the time. So, we've seen most of the shows in town. We went to see "Born Yesterday" this afternoon. She's been staying overnight with me the last few nights because my parents weren't here. Mr. Peyton let her take the car yesterday afternoon and last night we played Canasta and poker with Mr. & Mrs. Peyton — boy did I lose in poker. — I never could win in cards, and I was the only loser last night.

Gerrie & Doug sure would have liked to have you here when they were married — they mentioned it quite a few times.

The reception the Jones had for them was very nice. I guess they've told you all about everything so there's not much left to say about it. — How are you and the Army

The Opening Letters

Lila in 1951

getting along together Med? — I guess you're used to it now maybe. I hope it's not too rough Med.

Gerrie said you weren't in the infantry anymore. I couldn't figure out what you were in, but it sounded pretty good. I hope that it is better.

You should be very happy that you are where its warm — it's cold here right now. — It snowed almost all day. We haven't had much snow so far this winter — in fact it's been quite nice. Med, that sure is an address & a half you have, (A.P.O. right?) have you learned it yet? I haven't much left to say but I hope you're getting along okay.

And the Sergeants don't give you too bad a time.

Sincerely, Lila

Feb. 25, 1951

Hello Lila,

I received your very welcome letter the other day and was pleased to think you would write to me. It really does make a guy feel good to hear from his friends back home, as it means a great deal when your put away in a place like this. (Excuse that expression. I make it sound as though I was in prison.) But, due to the way we are treated I sometimes wonder if we have any more rights than the prisoners do and that's no kidding. If during the week we do the least little thing wrong, we are restricted for the weekend and can't go anyplace. In my opinion that is a method used to deal with children instead of men. But there isn't too much anyone can do about it, so will have to make the best of it. Although, last week we were good little boys, so they allowed us to go to El Paso, Texas, which is just seven miles away.

It did seem good just to get away from the camp and relax for a while. El Paso is a pretty nice city, but it also has its bad features, and I didn't have anything to do with them because it is easy to get into trouble there whether you want to or not. There are quite a few Mexican people there and as a rule they don't like Americans, (especially soldiers) so this sometimes causes a conflict. There has been any number of soldiers here get into trouble and that isn't good. If I am in the Army I might as well keep a clean slate. It might help sometime. You would be surprised as to the many ways a soldier can get into trouble, so it pays to keep on your toes.

Today is Sunday and I went to church this morning, which made me feel much better. I can see now how much the Gospel means to a person and it's for sure that it never does any harm. No kidding Lila, a friend of mine and I are the only two Mormons on the entire post. So, you can see we are outrated. They think our religion is kind of stupid, but most people do who don't understand it.

I guess Gerrie is awfully lonesome since Doug left, isn't she? I can well imagine how she feels, but there isn't much to do about it, so we will all have to make the best of it. I hope it isn't too long before we can all return to normal life again.

You mentioned something about losing in cards when you and Gerrie played with Mr. and Mrs. Peyton. Well, don't feel bad because every time I play cards here, I'm on the losing end regardless of how long we play. I guess we should have gotten together and learned how to play cards.

I spoke too soon about having good weather because this morning it was raining cats and dogs. I hope it doesn't turn for the worst and end up in a big snowstorm, which it sometimes does. But I could stand any of the weather down here after being in Kansas for so long. It was 20 degrees below zero the day we left there and believe me I was glad to get out of there.

Lila, are you still working at the Walker Bank? You are sure lucky; I wish I had your job, not only for the job, but for the money also. You know I only make $2.40 a day. Isn't that nice? A man can almost get by on that. I didn't think I would ever work for as little as that, but I have no choice in the matter. When I get to be a P.F.C. I will get a big raise of .35 cents per day. Nice huh?

Well anyway I'm glad that I'm not in the Infantry anymore. I am in the Anti-Aircraft-Artillery, which consists of the big guns used to fire at airplanes. I don't know too much about them yet except when they are fired it almost knocks you off your feet. Believe me they are noisy.

Medford 1951

Well Lila, it is almost time to go to bed and I can't think of much more to say. But no kidding Lila, I do appreciate your writing to me, and it did seem good to hear from you. I hope you will write again.

Sincerely yours,
Med

March 14, 1951

Dear Lila,

I received your last very welcome letter the other day and was most pleased to hear from you again. Like you said, the letters mean a great deal to a person when your so far away from home. I really do appreciate your writing to me Lila, as your letters help a great deal in cheering me up.

From the way I talked I guess you really got a horrible impression of the Army. I may have exaggerated somewhat, but all in all the Army just isn't any good as far as I'm concerned. I guess I am just to much of a home boy, as I always have been. It isn't to much the being away from home that bothers me, but it's the way

CHAPTER TWO

Basic Training

"No kidding, Lila, we are treated just like dirt under their feet. I didn't think I would ever have to take from anyone what I've had to take here, but there isn't much that can be done about it, so I may as well make the best of it."

March 14, 1951

Dear Lila,

 I received your last very welcome letter the other day and was most pleased to hear from you again. Like you said, the letters mean a great deal to a person when you are so far away from home. I really do appreciate your writing to me Lila, as your letters help a great deal in cheering me up.

 From the way I talked I guess you really got a horrible impression of the Army. I may have exaggerated somewhat, but all in all the Army just isn't any good as far as I'm concerned. I guess I am just too much of a home boy, as I have always been. It isn't too much the being away from home that bothers me, but also the way we are treated by our so-called superiors. No kidding, Lila, we are treated just like dirt under their feet. I didn't think I would ever have to take from anyone what I've had to take here, but there isn't much that can be done about it, so I may as well make the best of it. Like so many people have advised me, I can either make Army life more miserable than it really is by thinking that way, or try and make the most of it, like you said. Lately I have had a considerable change of attitude (for the better) so I do feel much better.

 Today we went on a twelve-mile hike out to the rifle range and believe it or not, I didn't even get tired. I am still trying to figure out how I ever walked so far without passing out or something, but I guess I am in much better condition than I thought. The heat was almost unbearable as it was 80 degrees today. That's quite warm for this time of the year don't you think? Although, we do have some terrible windstorms here, but as a rule the weather is mild all the time.

From the way you talked winter has finally hit Salt Lake. As much as I would like to be home, I think I would rather be down here for the winter than Salt Lake. I remember some of the terrible winters we used to have in Utah, and it sort of makes me feel good to know I am missing this one. But as much as I talk, I suppose I would jump at the chance if I could come home now.

I received a letter from Doug the other day and was glad to hear from him. I could tell that he doesn't think any more of the Army than I do. He naturally wouldn't, especially now that he and Gerrie are married. It really doesn't seem fair that they should take married men, but nothing seems to stop the Army from drafting. I was in hopes he would be sent somewhere near my camp, but apparently not. Well maybe I will run into him somewhere before I go overseas. We were promised a leave before going over and I am hoping it comes through.

The Page Cavanaugh Trio just got through playing on the radio. It sure makes me homesick, as I recall very distinctively the times I saw them at the Kasbah. Two girls also sang that song we liked so well, but I can't remember the name of it to save my soul. I probably won't sleep tonight, until I think of it.

Well, Lila, it is almost time for the lights to go out (9 o'clock) so I will have to close. I hope this letter doesn't bore you too much, as I haven't been able to think of anything to say tonight.

As Ever, Med

My company before we went on leave.

Med back row, second on right

Well, honey, I have been expecting a letter from you, but have not received one yet. But, I realize that the mail is in these Army camps very well because it takes so long to get one out of here. As yet, I haven't received any mail, so they must be delayed along the line somewhere. Honey, I hope you will write as often as possible because it means so much to me. It sure seemed good to hear your voice again when I called the other night. Although, I did have some trouble in hearing you plainly. I hope I didn't give you some wrong answer. I wanted to talk much longer, but the time is very short because there are so awfully many here and they all want to use the phones at the same time. You see, there are thousands of soldiers and they don't have facilities enough to handle half of them. It makes it miserable because whatever you do, no matter what, always a long line.

You know, Lila, sometimes I wonder how this government of ours gets along as well as it does because it

May 4, 1951

Hello: Lila,

Well, honey, I have been anxiously awaiting a letter from you, but have not received one yet. But, I realize how slow the mail is in these Army camps. I know very well because it takes two days to get one out of here. As yet, I haven't received any mail, so they must be delayed along the line somewhere. But, honey, I hope you will write as often as possible because it means so much to me. It sure seemed good to hear your voice again when I called you the other night. Although, I did have a little trouble in hearing you plainly and I hope I didn't give you some stupid answers. I wanted to talk to you longer, but the time is very limit-

---

CHAPTER THREE

Waiting For Deployment Orders

"But being away from you is
much worse than I ever dreamed it could be,
and all of this together is enough
to make a guy go crazy, but I guess
I will just have to control myself."

April 27, 1951

Hi-Honey,

Well, Lila, here I am sitting in the barracks at Camp Stoneman after a long and lonely ride, which I thought would never end. No kidding, honey, I may be here in body, but my heart is back home with you. I didn't think I could ever miss a person as much as I am missing you. Really, if I had known I was going to feel this way I would never have returned to the Army. I have thought about you constantly since my arrival here. It's getting so bad I can't even concentrate on my work, but I guess I will have to do my best to get over it for the time-being at least. Please, honey, don't think I am just feeding you a line or being too bold and forward, but I LOVE you very much and I am beginning to realize it more and more now that we can't see each other. Those two weeks I was home were the most enjoyable in my life and I only wish that we were together more during that time.

I know this may be asking a lot, but honey, will you please wait for me? The time does pass quite rapidly and before you know it I will be home again. It would please me very much if I knew that when I did return you would be there and not married to some other guy. I suppose you could tell that I felt this way all the time I was home, but the time did pass so rapidly, and we had to live so fast that I couldn't realize just then how much you really meant to me. Please, honey, think of me occasionally, for it will mean so very much to me. The Army hasn't been too good all along, but now it's much worse than I dreamed it could ever be. I just can't tell you how lonely and terrible I felt the night I bid you all goodbye, but I just hope I can spend my remaining time without doing something drastic, which I would regret later, for you are the most wonderful girl I have ever known, and it just can't be too long before I see you again. Honey, please forgive me if I acted sort of strange and upset the night I left because I just wasn't myself. I was so overcome with the idea of leaving that I just lost my head and if I said or did anything which didn't make sense to you or the folks, please forgive me.

Honey, why don't you call mom on the phone occasionally and talk to her? The folks do think a lot of you, and I know they would appreciate it very much to hear from you.

Well, kid, there isn't too much I can say about California because I haven't seen much yet, but what country I have seen is very beautiful. I don't know exactly, or when I will be leaving, but honey, I will write to you just as often as possible and there may be times when I can't get a letter through for a month or so, but all we can do is hope and pray for the best and I know everything will tun out alright. It just must, for I will be counting the days when I can see you again.

I have been separated from most of my friends including the guy from Morgan, Utah with whom I left, so you see why I don't feel so good about it. But being away from you is much worse than I ever dreamed it could be, and all of this together is enough to make a guy go crazy, but I guess I will just have to control myself.

I imagine you are seeing Gerrie regularly now huh? Be sure and tell her hello for me and I hope she isn't mad at me. Say hello to your mom and dad and your sisters. I think your parents are swell people and I hope they feel alright towards me, even though I did keep you out late.

Did you make it home in my car alright? That too is a worry and I hope the folks soon sell it. Maybe someday when this is over, I can buy a new one. Will you go for a ride with me? (Big joke huh?)

Well, honey, there isn't much more to say now except that I wrote you a card from Pittsburgh and it came back today because it wasn't properly addressed. But I wanted you to know anyhow. Please, write back real soon or I will go crazy and that's no kidding. I won't promise that this address is correct but write soon anyway and I am sure to get it eventually. I will close for now, but will write again soon.

With Lots of Love to the sweetest girl I ever have known,

Sincerely,
Med

May 4, 1951

Hello Lila,

    Well honey, I have been anxiously awaiting a letter from you, but have not received one yet. But I realize how slow the mail is in these Army camps. I know very well because it takes two days to get one out of here. As yet, I haven't received any mail, so they must be delayed along the line somewhere. But, honey, I hope you will write as often as possible because it means so much to me. It sure seemed good to hear your voice again when I called you the other night. Although, I did have a little trouble in hearing you plainly and I hope I didn't give you some stupid answers. I wanted to talk to you longer, but the time is very limited because there are so awfully many soldiers here and they all want to use the phones at the same time. No kidding, there are thousands of soldiers here and they don't have facilities enough to handle half of them, which really makes it miserable because anything you do, no matter what, there is always a long line.

    You know, Lila, sometimes I wonder just how this government of ours gets along as well as it does because if they handled everything like they do the Army it would be no time at all until we had a revolution. No kidding, honey, everything here is in such a turmoil and complete state of confusion that I just don't know which end my head is on and I don't think the big wheels do either. It makes me so damn mad because I could just as well have had another two weeks at home for all the good I am doing here. So far, I haven't done one thing of importance other than K. P. and details every day. I will probably spend another week here doing nothing but just waiting for orders and to think I could just as well have been home seeing you, which means everything to me.

This morning all my buddies were shipped out, including the one I left with, and here I am all alone and no orders yet. Honey, I have never felt so all alone in my life because I don't know a soul. I just wish to hell that I had shipped out this morning with the rest of them because it does mean so much to a guy to be with someone he knows and can trust. Maybe, by chance, some more will ship in here whom I know, and I sure hope so. Honey, if only you were here – that's all that matters, but I guess that's just wishful thinking, which I hadn't better do too much of at the present time, at least, or I might decide to take off and come home regardless of the consequences. No kidding, I would just as soon ship out now and get it over with because I must go anyway and the longer I wait the longer it will be before I get home again.

Lila, I suppose you get tired if me complaining of the Army all the time, but I just can't help it and I would give anything in the world if I could get home and see you again. Everything I said before still goes and always will – I only hope that you think of me as much as I think of you.

When you talk to the folks again don't tell them that I told you I was going to Korea because it would only worry them – especially Mom - and with her physical condition the way it is, it might not do her too much good. Honey, I wish I hadn't told you that either, but I said it before I realized what I was saying and maybe I won't go there after all. Let's hope and pray I don't.

Say hello to your folks for me and anybody else who might be in the least bit interested as to my whereabouts. Honey, please forgive me if I sound as though I might be tee-ed off tonight, but I'm not – just upset because they separated me from all my friends.

Well, Lila, it is almost time for bed, so I had better close for now. Please write real often, as I won't sleep well until I hear from you. You be good and take care of yourself and I will write again soon.

I love you lots –

Sincerely,
Med

May 8, 1951

My Dearest Lila,

Well honey, I received your most wonderful letter today and no kidding, Lila, there just aren't words enough to express the way I felt while reading it. I have read it so many times that the paper is almost worn out. It made me feel oh! so much better to hear from you and it seemed almost as though you were right here talking to me. And to think that you once told me you couldn't write letters. Honey, that was the most beautiful letter I ever read, and it couldn't have been worded more perfectly. They told me at the mail room that the letter came last Saturday, but I was on K. P. all day and didn't even get a chance to pick up my mail. Had I known that your letter was there I would have torn the place down to get it. Honey, I will always keep that letter and wherever I go it will go also. It means that very much to me. Lila, it makes me so happy to know that you feel the way you do. I told you before and I will say it again – "I love you so much," and I realize it more and more every day. Honey, I am running around her in a daze because my thoughts are constantly with you and I am finding it difficult to keep my mind on anything else, but I suppose I had better try to concentrate on the Army a little more because it might be for my own good.

Honey, everything we learn from here on out will be of the upmost importance, so I guess I had better try to absorb all the knowledge I can, even though I don't have any more interest in the Army now than the man in the moon. I always did hate the Army but now I just can't explain how much I detest everything about it.

I miss you so much – and yet I can't see you. That's what seems so hard to understand. Honey, I don't think I could feel any worse if I were locked up in prison, for you at least could come and see me from time to time. This way I may not see you for a year and honey, that's a long time when you feel the way I do. But I am sure everything will work out – and receiving that wonderful letter from you has given me so much more faith and courage, which I need very much. Lila, I am afraid and I'm not ashamed to admit it. Everyone is when they are told of going into combat, even old-timers from the last war. I was talking with one today and he said, "if ever we have to fight again there will still be that certain fear in our hearts, which possesses every man."

Honey please don't pay too much attention to the way I talk, for I may never see action, but if I do, I want to prepare myself because they say, "the biggest battle will be with yourself" and I can believe that very much.

May 9, 1951

Well Lila, just when I was getting a good start on this letter some damn Sgt. came in and said I had been chosen to go on guard duty, so that put a stop to my finishing this letter yesterday. No kidding honey, I walked guard off and on all night and then the dirty so-and-so's wouldn't even let me sleep this morning. I am really worn out, but finishing this letter is more important than sleeping anyway.

Honey, I received your second wonderful letter yesterday and was really thrilled to hear from you again. I don't feel near so bad now that your letters are getting through to me. I am still awfully lonely because they are shipping out the last two fellows of our outfit with whom I came down here and after they go, I won't know one person in this company. It makes me so damn mad to think they are keeping me here so long because I must spend so much time overseas anyway and the sooner they ship me out the sooner I will get home again. Honey, I am looking forward to that day with all my heart in order that we may be together again. Believe me, Lila, I will never go overseas again once I get home – no matter what they do to me, as I am going to take you up on that idea of kidnapping me. Ha!

Well honey, it was sure nice to hear all the news from home and I hope you will be able to keep me posted as much as possible. I think it's a very good idea that you and the folks are keeping in touch with each other when you receive mail for then no one will have to worry because one of you will for sure get a letter without having to wait very long.

Honey, I am very proud of you for donating a pint of blood and I do hope you don't have any aftereffects. You know I have seen people pass out and become very ill at least a day or so after giving blood, but like you said honey, maybe you were too fascinated to notice it very much. I guess the people that do get sick are weaklings, but honey you seem to be in very good health. Listen to me, honey, I am not trying to frighten you from giving any more – just don't pay attention to me. And Lila, I am very proud of you because your donation does mean so very much. And just think, it may save my life some day or some other beat-out soldier's life.

Lila it was very sweet of you to want me to tell you if I ever need anything. Really, there isn't too much I will need, for I have received a partial payment and that will keep me in what few articles I need for a long time. But honey, if I ever do need something which might be hard to get maybe you could send it and I would appreciate it so much.

You know honey, I haven't even tried to get a pass yet in order that I might go to some nearby town because if you weren't there with me, I know I wouldn't enjoy it. For honey, I got so used to having you with me while I was home that I just couldn't go any place now and really have fun. I pray to God that it won't be very long before I get home because I have so much to come back to – You, my wonderful parents and family and friends. You know Lila, I do have a very strong desire and will of getting home before long and I just know it will be.

As I am sitting here writing this letter Patti Page is singing "Would I Love You" on the radio and honey, there's something about that song that seems to cut right through me because we did hear it so much while I was home, and it reminds me so much of the wonderful moments we spent together. I wish I had a recording of it, for I would play it all night.

Lila, I will call you again before I go and it was sweet of you to want me to reverse the charges, but really it doesn't cost that much, and I will probably receive more money before leaving. I can't say when I will call, but it should be sometime next week, and I hope our connection is better as I want to remember your voice just as it really is because it may be a long time before I hear it again.

You know Lila, I remember how we used to sit in my car and talk, and that certain sweet smile on your face that I will never forget – and I don't want to because it does me so much good to just imagine that you were here. I love you so much and wish that I were home with you, but I would rather be a soldier with love than without it because there is always such a wonderful feeling and memories which help very much to keep you going.

Med and Lila

Honey, I'm not worried about you going out – and if you do, if you feel the way you do, there isn't anything to worry about. You should go out because I know how tiresome it is to stay home. But honey, that is entirely up to you to decide and really, I won't worry if you do go out occasionally. Like I said before, "you are the most wonderful girl I have ever gone with" and I will always think so and admire you for so many things.

Lila, thanks for telling me all the news in your letters and I can't even attempt to write about all of it, but I think I have covered most of the important phases.

I am glad that Gerrie isn't mad at us anymore because Doug's and her friendship means an awful lot to me, and I am sure it does to you also. Tell her hello for me. I received a letter from Doug today, but it was written a month ago and I can't imagine what has delayed it for so long. It was good to hear from him again.

I have written the folks two letters and hope they received them because they do worry so much, especially mom. We have lost two in our family you know and if anything happened to me – that would probably finish mom. Excuse me honey, here I go again talking like a damn fool. I don't know why I talk so stupid and there really isn't anything to worry about yet.

I hope you don't get bored reading this letter, for it is a long one and probably all mixed up because I have written so much. I haven't been able to write for a few days so I thought I would write a longer letter.

You know honey, I haven't written my brother since I have been here, and I feel like hell about it, so I guess I better sneak in a few lines tonight. I suppose he and Nellie wonder what has happened to me.

Well honey, you take good care of yourself, and I hope you don't worry because everything is alright, except that I'm lonely and miss you so very much. Tell your folks hello.

I'll be loving you always,

Sincerely,

Med

P.S. Write real soon

Well, Lila, here I am
  ancing up and down so
 the middle of the Paci
 ... You know, honey, I
 ...e the world was co
 much water. For t...
 now all I have see
 ... and believe me I ...
 ...ed to see land aga...
 though, it will be
 ...ve often heard people
 ... sea sickness but
 ...ed it could make a p
 ...lutely sick. No kid
 ..., the first three days

CHAPTER FOUR

Boarding Ship in San Francisco, USNS Sgt. H.E. Woodford

"Honey, I love you so much
that I can hardly stand it, and this
is one day of my life which I will
never forget, for I know it's
going to be a long time before I see
you again."

May 14, 1951

My Dearest Lila,

Well honey, I don't have access to any writing paper at the present time so thought I would sneak in a few lines on this picture. I don't know whether the picture will mean much to you honey but anyway this is the ship I will board in San Francisco and will take me to Japan – I hope. I am now on a harbor boat crossing the bay and should sail sometime tonight.

Lila, I am so happy that I was able to call you Saturday. You just don't realize how much it meant to me, for I wanted to hear your voice just once more and I will never forget it. Honey, I love you so much that I can hardly stand it, and this is one day of my life which I will never forget, for I know it's going to be a long time before I see you again. Lila, I'll live for the day when we can be together again, and my only wish is that it won't be too long before that can be.

Honey, my sister and brother-in-law came to see me yesterday and I finally got a pass, so they proceeded to show me a good time. However, I didn't enjoy anything because you weren't with me. We could have had such a wonderful time together yesterday, but I just know that someday, maybe not too long from now, we can be together again. Well honey, tell everyone hello and I will write as soon as possible.

I love you with all my heart,

Med

May 26, 1951 — Saturday

Hi – Honey,

 Well Lila I am bouncing up and down somewhere in the middle of the Pacific Ocean. You know honey, I didn't realize the world was composed of so much water. For twelve days now all I have seen is water and believe me I will be glad to see land again, even though it will be Japan. I have often heard people talk about seasickness, but I never realized it could make a person so deathly sick. No kidding honey, the first three days I thought I was going to die, and it was only yesterday that I began to feel normal again. They told us to try and eat as much as possible but really, I couldn't hold anything down for three days, but now I have acquired an appetite again and feel so much better. I think the reason for being sick so long is because of the numerous storms we have run in to along the way. You know honey, one day the water would be nice and calm and then we would run into a storm, which would toss the ship around so much that it felt almost as though we would tip over – and these are the times when I really became ill.

 Well honey I guess there isn't much sense in complaining again as you know very well how I feel, but Lila, I want you to know that you haven't left my mind once since we departed from the states and instead of only twelve days it seems like twelve long years that I have been gone. I realize now that I had better adjust myself to being away from you because it will be a good long time yet before we will see each other and my being miserable depends entirely upon me. I am trying to look on the brighter side of things – if there are any. If only there could have been someone with me whom I know and could talk to, but there isn't and that's why I have felt so lonely. I have talked to a few guys, but they just don't seem as friendly and easy to get along with as those whom I trained with and have known for so long. I am sure hoping that I will be able to see some of my buddies when I reach Japan.

You know honey, I should have known better than to tell you I could get a letter off this ship because we have gone right through without a single stop, so you see I haven't had a chance to mail any letters. I suppose you and the folks have wondered what happened to me, but I did send you a picture of the beat-up ship and I also wrote a few lines – hope you received them.

You know Lila, your letters have been a great consolation to me, for I have read them over and over so many times that they are almost worn out (and that's no kidding). I can't hardly wait until I receive more from you because they do mean so very much to me. You know honey, receiving letters from someone you love and yearn (crude expression) to be with does more than anything in the world to lift the gloom and help cheer you up, no matter how far apart you might be. Right now, we are about 3,500 miles from San Francisco and by the

U.S. Army Transport Sgt. Howard E. Woodford
sailing on to Korea

time we reach our destination it will be over 4,500 miles away. Honey, if I can receive letters from you, it won't seem much different than being somewhere in the states.

Well doll, tonight is Saturday and how I wish I were home with you having fun like we did when I was home, but they are showing a movie tonight so I guess I will go. It will, at least, take my mind off this tiresome and boring journey, which I hope will end soon. Honey, I will write more tomorrow, and I hope I am inspired so I can write something of more interest. (Big joke huh?)

May 27, 1951

Sunday

Hello! Honey –

Well, here it is Sunday morning and the starting of another day, but I do feel pretty good because it is a beautiful day and the water is just as calm and smooth as glass, which is really quite a relief after a rough and stormy night. I have found out that we will reach our destination sometime tomorrow so as soon as possible I will mail this letter, but it will probably take two weeks to reach you. Honey, I hope you noticed my overseas address on the last letter, in which I sent a picture of the ship, as I forgot to tell you, but it will be on this letter also, so be sure to copy it correctly. I hope it isn't too long before I can hear from you honey, because I am awfully anxious to know how you're getting along – I worry about you very much. I know there isn't any reason to worry but you know me, Lila. Maybe it's because of my love and affection for you that makes me feel that way.

Honey, I guess there isn't anything much of importance I can write about pertaining to this trip except that us poor enlisted men are still getting a raw deal. There are several officers on the ship with us and believe it or not they have been taking showers in fresh clean water and we have had scarcely enough to drink. Isn't that a dirty deal? And, if we so desire to shower or shave, we do it in cold salt water. Not only that but the officers have their own private staterooms and almost all the comforts of home while we are crammed down in the galleys like so many sardines crowded in a tin can. Honestly honey, we have been so crowded and pushed around I almost felt like jumping overboard. And then to see these officers running around with that look of arrogance on their faces – it makes me so damn mad that I feel like punching one of them in the nose, but I suppose I hadn't better try that. Here I go again – honey, you probably think I am a communist or something, but it is the truth. I have made up my mind that I can take anything, they throw at me because I know that someday I will be out of this mess, and I am looking forward to that day with all my heart. (For more reasons than one).

Well honey, when you write be sure to tell me all the news – how your job has been going and what you have been doing. (Lila, you don't have to answer that last remark. I guess I am getting too personal, but I really didn't mean it that way.) Honey, you just tell me anything you think I should know.

How do you like the car by now? Once you have gotten used to a car of your own it's hard to do without one – how well I know. But Lila, I hope you did get a good one because that is the most important thing and when you drive around the block, please think of me and how I wish I were with you.

Lila, I have concluded that when I get "over there" I won't have the time and opportunity to write to all my friends, so honey, if you see any of them will you please tell them I am alright and will write if I can. If I can write to you and my immediate family – that's all that matters anyway.

How is Gerrie getting along? Did she finally get settled with her job situation? If you know anything about Doug, would you please tell me as I haven't heard from him for so long.

Well lover, I hope this poorly constructed letter will make sense to you because it really doesn't to me. I have written it rather hurriedly and I know it's all jumbled up, but honey, I tried anyways and if I had time, I know I could have done better, but in the Army, there is no such thing as time. I will write again just as soon as I get situated in Japan and honey, please write real soon as I will be looking forward to your most wonderful letters, for they seem to bring us so much nearer each other and "doll", that's the way I want to feel. If there are times when you don't hear from me too often, please don't think it isn't because I don't want to write, for it does give me so much pleasure to be able to write to you and I will – just as often as possible.

Say hello to everyone for me and I hope you are keeping in contact with my folks. I am going to write them today also. Be good honey, and take care of yourself, for I want to see you again – just as cute and sweet as the day I left you.

Loving and missing you always,
'Your boy' – I hope! Med

P.S. If only you could see me now. I've had all my hair cut off.

May 29, 1951 — Tuesday

Camp Drake, Japan

My Dearest Lila,

Well honey, we arrived at Yakohama last night at 9:00 pm. After being up all night without a wink of sleep we are finally getting situated in our new camp, which is located just 17 miles from Tokyo. It is called Camp Drake. Honey, as far as I know we will be here only a short time – maybe a day or so and after that I cannot say. Most of the men here have been going to Korea, but honey, I am putting every ounce of faith and trust in the Lord that I won't be sent there. I will receive my orders this afternoon so keep your fingers crossed for me. I didn't want to tell you this, but if I am sent there you would have to know sooner or later, so I thought I would tell you now.

We sure received a most wonderful reception from the Japanese people when we pulled into the bay last night. They had an Army Band playing for our benefit and people cheering. For the first time during my Army career, I felt a certain proudness in my heart – proud to be an American and oh, how I miss the good old United States and you honey, more than ever before. If only I could have seen your sweet face among those spectators, it would have made me feel so much better. Maybe someday when I return to the states you can be there to see me.

You know darling, last night as we were riding out here on the train and I was in one of my depressed and melancholy moods as usual, they passed out to us all our delayed mail that had been sent to Camp Stoneman and honey, I received four letters from you, one from the folks and one from Dick and Nellie. Lila, I just can't express to you how wonderful and relieved I felt to get all those letters from you. They mean so much to me and it seems as though everyone gets better, and I am so happy to know how you feel towards me. I hope and pray nothing will change that, for honey, I guess you know too how I feel towards you and my love and devotion for you grows more each day. Wherever I go and whatever hardships I may have to undergo I will always carry in my heart an unending love for you. Honey, I also received your beautiful picture and how happy and thrilled I was to get it, as I have been awaiting it for a long time. Honey you sure do look sweet and thanks a million. That picture will go with me wherever I might be sent and how wonderful I will feel when I am thinking of you and can have that sweet picture to look at.

Lila, I can't begin to write about everything you covered in all those letters but honey it was so good to hear all the news and please do keep writing just as many and as often as you possibly can. They are all I've got to look forward to now that I am so far away from you.

Lila, there isn't much I can tell you about Japan yet because I haven't seen much and we would have to go through Tokyo after dark, but I imagine I will see plenty before I leave here. The weather here is very nice and quite like that of California, so I am glad for that.

Honey, my time is very limited today and I've had to write this in just 15 minutes so if there is something which you can't understand or if it seems stupid, please forgive me as I didn't even get time to read it over. The folk's letter and my brothers were also very nice and I had better try and write them a few lines today because they do worry so much, especially mom. Dad said in his letter that they are very favorably impressed with you, and I knew they would be. How could anyone help but like you Lila?

Well honey, I will have to close for now, but will write more tomorrow or the next day. My address will remain the same until further notified. I am alright and please don't worry too much about me. Say hello to everyone for me and write real often. Take good care of yourself darling.

With My Deepest of Love,

Med

P.S. Pray for me, honey.

Med's Family
Garland (Dick) and Nellie Poulson
(brother & wife on left);
Beth and Henry Oliver Poulsen
(mother & father on right)

Boarding Ship in San Francisco, USNS Sgt. H.E. Woodford

Lila

CHAPTER FIVE

Destination: Korea

"One of the guys saw it and asked me how
    I rated to know a sweet looking girl
like you and honey, how right he is
        because you are a sweet girl, and
    you mean the world to me and how
I am going to fight and work for the
        day we will be together again."

May 30, 1951 — Thursday

Dearest Lila,

    Well honey, I received my orders this morning and will be shipping out tonight or in the morning. My destination will be Korea, but I don't know yet whether I will be assigned to a AAA Unit or Infantry, and I probably won't know until I get there.

    Oh Lila, how I've hoped and prayed I wouldn't be sent there, but I guess it has all been in vain. I have always been unlucky, and it looks as though luck won't change because half of the guys are going to Korea and the other half will remain here and I would be in the bunch to leave. But darling, I'm not going to give up yet and Lila, please pray for me because that is the only thing that will help now. If we put our faith and trust in God – He will just have to hear us and bring me home safely. I have so much to live for and look forward to (meaning you) that nothing will happen – it just can't. Honey, I have decided to try and not worry too much if I can help it because there is so much to worry about and so many formalities to go through that a person might crack up if he lets himself go, and it has happened.

    This has been a busy day, for they have been pushing and rushing around so much that I hardly know which end my head is on. We have been processing all day and I'm lucky to have been able to get this letter written, but honey I'll write to you no matter how busy I am. You know Lila, they have taken all our personal belongings away from us because we don't have any means by which to carry them, but they will never get your pictures and letters away from me because I consider them more important than even my equipment and I know I will spend many a lonely night in Korea – how nice it will be to have your wonderful letters to read. If I don't have them I know I will go crazy.

Honey, I received the larger picture of you yesterday and how happy I was to receive it. Lila, you sure, look sweet and thanks a million – I'll cherish and carry the picture with me wherever I go. One of the guys saw it and asked me how I rated to know a sweet looking girl like you and honey, how right he is because you are a sweet girl, and you mean the world to me and how I am going to fight and work for the day we will be together again.

Darling, they are making us go to bed early tonight, as we must get up at 4:30 in the morning and be ready to ship out. We are going by train which will take about 36 hours and Lila, I'll try my best to write you again while I'm on the train. They also told us we wouldn't receive any more mail until we reach our destination but honey, please keep writing real often as they will always catch up to me. I probably won't have time to write to the folks or my brother tonight but will try tomorrow and if they are not hearing from me too often will you please tell them I am alright, and not to worry.

Honey, I suppose I will have to tell them I am going to Korea because they are bound to find out sooner or later and I hope mom doesn't take it too hard, but I am afraid she will. I guess the best thing to do would be to tell her I am still in the Anti-Aircraft, and I know she will feel better about that.

Well dearest, I don't have any more time tonight, so I better close. Honey, don't worry too much yet because I am not quite certain what sort of deal I will get and whatever it is, I will do my best to safeguard my life because I am always thinking of the day we will meet again. Be a good kid and may God bless you and keep you always.

With all my Love,

Your boy, Med

Lila

June 1, 1951 — Friday

Sasebo, Japan

My Darling Lila,

Hi ya doing honey? I don't have much time tonight, but I am going to write this letter regardless of what I must do.

Well honey, after a 36-hour train ride from Camp Drake, I am now in Sasebo, Japan which is another replacement center and the last camp I will be in before going to Korea. Sasebo is located on the northern shore of Japan, and we will leave here sometime tomorrow. Oh, Lila if I could just see you once more before I go – how relieved and comforted I would feel, but I do have your cute pictures to look at and honey, I've been looking at them all day. They do make me feel so much better and it seems almost as though you could speak to me. Someday Lila, I will hear your voice again and how I am praying it won't be too long. I love you with all my heart and nothing can ever change that. Wherever I go and how long I might be gone my thoughts and prayers will ever be of you. How I wish I could have met you long before I had to come in the Army. Honey, we didn't have much time to be together and I didn't realize how much you really meant to me until I came home on that last leave. I just can't make myself believe it's true that I must be so far from you.

Oh, how I wish I could awaken and find this is all

a horrible nightmare. Honey, I just can't seem to get it out of my mind the idea of going into combat – how will I react and what's going to happen? All I have heard in our orientations the past few days is Kill! Kill! or be killed and it's weighing on my mind so much that I feel as though I will go crazy. Oh, why do I have to be here? It all seems so utterly stupid and senseless, but that is the question nobody can answer. Honey, I'm not a coward and I am sure there are thousands of other soldiers who feel the same, so please don't think I am a big baby or something. I'll fight, honey, for all I'm worth because thinking of you, I know, will give me added faith and courage which I'm going to need very much. Please keep praying for me honey, and I know all our prayers won't be in vain. I know I shouldn't be talking the way I am but honey, I want you to know, and I just had to get it off my chest.

I haven't received any more of your letters the past few days, but I am sure they will catch up to me. Please write as often or every day if you can because they are going to mean more to me now than ever before. Honey, I know you will so I shouldn't keep saying that. Lila, I know I haven't been writing to the folks as much maybe as I should, but will you tell them to write more often if they can? There are three letters on the way to them now, so they shouldn't worry if they think I am not writing. I finally wrote to Jay today after so long a time (he's the fellow that lived next door to me – remember?)

He has always been one of my best friends, so I thought I should write. I also wrote to Walt Larson. There are more friends of mine I would like to write to, but I just don't have the time and honey, I want to write you at every opportunity possible, so that's why I don't have time to write everyone else.

    I tried to get another letter to Doug also, but it was returned, and I don't know why because it was addressed properly. Honey, if you know anything about him will you please tell me? I am awfully anxious to know what he is doing after not hearing from him for so long.

    Honey, I hope everything is going alright with you and the rest of your family. I suppose the bank is keeping you pretty busy huh? It seemed that way in your letter.

    Gee honey, I wish I could be home during the summer months, at least. I just love the summertime in good old Salt Lake – there are so many things we could do. But darling, I am looking forward to next summer and maybe, by chance, I might be discharged by then. Let's hope.

    Well honey, I hate to stop writing but there isn't much more time now before I go to bed and tomorrow, I will be bound for Korea. I just can't quit thinking about it. I wrote three previous letters before this one, all in the past few days. Lila, I sure hope you receive them. I won't get any more of yours until I reach my destination, but I hope they get there soon.

Be good darling, and once again I say – "I'm loving and missing you more each day." With best wishes to my sweet girl.

Sincerely,

Med

P.S. Say hello to Gerrie.

June 3, 1951 — Sunday

Pusan, Korea

Darling Lila,

Well honey, it's me again and I have finally reached this dreaded 'hole' of Korea and Lila, that's all it is, believe me. I just couldn't believe my eyes that such conditions of filth and rot could exist in the world. Honey, I have heard several guys talk of the conditions here, but you just couldn't conceive of anything so terrible until you see it for yourself. I don't see how they can live in such filth, and their food is rotten. That is one thing they (officers) have stressed very strongly to us – "don't eat any Korean food no matter how hungry you might get" – and I am sure they needn't tell us anymore because the sight and odor of it makes you sick. Also, the people are the same. I don't think most of them have had a bath in twenty years and honey, their clothing is just terrible, as you will see them dressed in anything they can get their hands on and some of the children don't wear any clothing at all. I just can't begin to tell you how disgusting and rotten it really is. The Army doctors have told us that Korea is the most disease-infested place on earth and they didn't exaggerate one bit.

You know Lila, since I last saw you, I have received 12 shots and vaccinations and now I can see how important they really are because if we didn't receive them, we would be subject to catch most any disease on earth. After seeing all this honey, it makes me appreciate more and more the fact that I am an American and can live in a land of prosperity and freedom for all. I can just imagine what would happen to America if it ever fell into the hands of the communists – we would be living just as they do here and honey, I would rather die first and I know most all the guys here feel the same way. I am beginning to see now the importance of this war and how much it means to all of us to win! I'll do my part, and how I'm looking forward to the day I can come back to you and talk about this thing as a past experience and it is honey, one which I will never forget.

Darling, you mean more to me than anything on earth and I want you to know that thinking of you is giving me faith and courage to see this thing through. I WILL come back honey. I know that now, but it is going to take time. Our commanding officer here told us that the rotation plan is in its full effectiveness now, so I should get out of here sometime in November – that is if the situation doesn't get any worse. So, honey, that is good news and something to look forward to – don't you think?

I don't think we will be here more than two or three days (Pusan). After that we will move up closer to the front, I imagine. Honey, I have been assigned to the famous 7th Infantry Division, which has been doing a marvelous job in Korea. Remember the name of my outfit and when you hear of it, think of me and that I am taking a part of whatever is going on. Lila, I can't say yet whether I will be in the Anti-Aircraft or just the Infantry, but keep your fingers crossed and let's pray for the best.

Honey, I haven't seen any of my buddies from home or any whom I trained with, but I am getting used to that now, and I am sure I will make new friends.

I hope you are doing alright as usual, and honey don't work too hard. We were told that we wouldn't receive any more mail probably for a month or so, but I hope this isn't true, for I don't know how long I can go without hearing from you. Darling, your letters mean all in the world to me and I'll bet I will have plenty of them when they do finally get here. This makes five I have written to you in the past few days – hope you receive them. I doubt very much if the address will be correct on this one, as we haven't received our final one yet, but Lila, please use it and I know they will get to me sooner or later.

Well kid, I really must close for now, but will write as often as is permitted. Say hello to everyone for me and honey, don't worry too much about me because I am alright so far, and I'm sure I will continue to be so. With best wishes and everlasting love to you, and I say this with all sincerity.

As Always Before,

Med

June 8, 1951 — Friday (I think)
Korea

My Darling Lila,

    Well honey, it's been almost a week since I have written to you and believe me, I just haven't been able to. No kidding honey, I have traveled and seen so much in the last two weeks that I hardly know which end my head is on. Really Lila, I have lost all track of time and I have been blotted out from the entire world. But darling, as long as my thoughts can be of you things don't seem quite so bad and Lila, they are, and always will as long as I live. Honey, I just can't find words to tell you how much I love you and how very much I think of you. Oh Lila, if you only knew how I feel – and I keep telling myself, why do I have to be away from you? It just doesn't make sense, but honey, how I am hoping and praying this terrible thing will soon end.

155MM Howitzer, Korea

Honey, in the last few letters I have written you (and I hope you received them) I have been all excited about being part of the Infantry, but Lila, the last minute they changed my orders again and I have been assigned to the 31st Field Artillery, which is a much better deal (I hope). The artillery always stays behind the front lines about 4-5 miles at least, and that's where I am now. But honey, believe me, that is as close as I ever want to be, and I have already seen some of the terrible horrors of the war. Lila, there are several things I could tell you, but I think it's best that I don't because I don't want to worry you. And darling, please don't worry too much because I am alright, and I don't think I will be in too much danger – let's hope not anyway.

Honey, I still haven't received any of your mail for at least two weeks, but I am hoping they will soon catch up to me because I will feel so much better when I can hear from you. Honey, my thoughts are always of you, and I've just got to hear from you before very long.

Lila, I have been told that the Artillery doesn't get rotated nearly as quick as the Infantry, and I may be here a year but honey, that won't matter if I know you will be there when I return. Darling, I know it is a long time for you to wait, but you are all in the world I want and I'm just living for the day I'll be with you again.

Lila, if I don't get a chance to write to the folks before you receive this letter, please tell them I am alright and give them this address, as it is my final one. Darling, please, hurry and write back using this address because your letters will get here much quicker than before. I just can't wait until I hear from you.

Well honey, I can't write much more tonight because we are moving our guns to new positions where we will be able to get better fire control on the Gooks (Chinese). Honestly honey, we have been killing them like flies, but they continue to come. Lila, the field artillery consists of the big guns they use to support the Infantry and believe me they are noisy.

Honey, I'll write as often as possible, and you do the same. Please tell my folks not to worry and I'll write whenever possible. I hope everything is O.K. with you honey and take good care of yourself. Tell everyone hello for me. Please don't worry.

With all my love to you, darling.
Your boy, Med

4th Gun Section, North Korea

LOVE LETTERS FROM HEARTBREAK RIDGE

Destination: Korea

> June 16, 1951
> North, Korea
>
> Hi - Honey,
>
> Well, Lila, it's me again and I'm still here, as much as I hate to say it. I've been here almost two weeks now and believe me honey, it seems more like two long, horrible years. The time goes by so awfully slow and not only that, but I am working much harder than I have

CHAPTER SIX

Front Line, North Korea

"The reason they said they picked me for the job as loader is because I look strong and husky, but if they only knew."

June 16, 1951

North Korea

Hi Honey,

    Well Lila, it's me again and I'm still here, as much as I hate to say it. I've been here almost two weeks now and believe me honey, it seems more like two long, horrible years. The time goes by so awfully slow and not only that, but I am working much harder than I have ever done in my life. Honey, I know a little work isn't going to hurt me, but the work is so heavy and strenuous that it's almost all I can do. The shells which we fire in the gun weigh almost 100 lbs. and I must throw them in as fast as I can and believe me after an hour or so of that I feel almost as though I would drop. Here I go complaining again and there isn't any way to get out of this outfit so I may as well shut up, but I thought I would let you know what I am doing. I guess I shouldn't feel too bad because it is much better than the infantry and after all that does mean a lot. The reason they said they picked me for the job as loader is because I look strong and husky, but if they only knew.

    You know honey, after one month vacation, which I had, I am in a run-down condition and it's hard to be able to do heavy work again. Also, the terrific noise the guns make when fired is almost unbearable and I only hope it doesn't affect my eardrums, which it has done to several fellows. The other day one fellow was standing too close behind it and the terrible concussion when fired knocked him down. Honey, I'm not telling you this to worry you, but I have thought I might as well let you know what's going on and I am sure that if I watch myself carefully everything will be O.K.

Lila, we sure have advanced a long way since I came to Korea and right now, we are approximately 30 miles above the 38th Parallel in central North Korea. Things seem to be going smooth as we are advancing quite rapidly and not meeting too much resistance from the Gooks (Chinese). However, we have had a few minor contacts with them while moving our guns to new positions, but nothing very serious. I only hope it will continue to be so.

You know darling, it's amazing how much damage these big guns can do because only two hours ago, we fired five rounds (shells) at the enemy and destroyed three of their vehicles and killed 50 men. They were almost ten miles away and we can still hit them with accuracy, so you see what a vital part the artillery plays in the war, and I haven't told you anything yet. Honey, you probably wonder how we can tell what damage we are doing being so far away from the enemy, but we have ground and air observers on the front lines who contact us by radio and tell us what we are doing. Well, I guess I have said enough of the war news for now, but I wanted you to know what I am doing because you have probably been wondering what I am up to. You know honey, there is an old saying that after two weeks in combat you are an old soldier and believe me, I feel like one. My only wish is that my six months will pass by in a hurry so I can get home and see you again.

Oh Lila, if you only knew how much I think of you and yearn to be home with you, and I hope and pray that nothing will happen and interfere with our seeing each other again. Honey, I didn't think I could ever love and miss a person as much as you and it is a wonderful feeling because it does give me added faith and courage to withstand any hardships which I might face. Darling, it may be a year or even more and I'm looking forward to that day with all my heart and believe it or not I have even been counting the days, but there are so many that I gave up.

Well honey, as yet I haven't received any mail from you and it's been almost three weeks, but I have moved around so much that it will take quite some time for your letters to reach me, but after they once get started, I should receive them quite rapidly. I just can't wait until I get them because your letters are the only thing I must look forward to over here. Honey, I have been writing to you quite often as possible and I do hope you have been getting them. I have also written the folks lately so if they don't receive them, you be sure and tell them won't you honey?

I guess there really isn't much more to say for now but say hello to everyone for me and you take good care of yourself and don't work too hard. I'll write soon again and please, don't worry.

With all my love to you honey,
Med

P.S. It's still raining here, and I have been drenched for the past three days, but I should be getting used to that now.

July 7, 1951
North Korea

Hello Honey,

I have a couple few spare minutes so I thought I would write a few lines and let you know that everything is still O.K. Darling, believe me when I say I'm sorry and feel badly because I haven't been able to write more often lately, but honey, I just haven't had the chance. Lila, I know this is a one-sided affair because you have been writing ten letters to my one, but I do hope you will understand that under the circumstances I just don't have the time and opportunity to write many letters. Honey, I do enjoy writing to you, and I would write every day, if possible, but time just doesn't permit.

In the past few days honey, I have received five more of your most wonderful letters. Oh honey, if I could just tell you how very much they mean to me and what a comforted feeling I get each time I read one – there just aren't words enough to express my feelings. If I could just take you in my arms and kiss you for every letter I receive, I'm sure you would understand the love and affection I have for you. Reading your letters honey seems to bring us so much closer and at times I even imagine I can hear your voice talking to me. I have read each one of them at least a dozen times and by doing that, it seems to be the only thing that keeps me going when I get in one of those depressed and melancholy moods, which are quite frequent with me lately, even more-so than ever. You know Lila, I thought as time goes on, I would become adjusted to being away from you, for the time being at least, but that just doesn't seem to be working out that way and my every thought is of you and home. The only thing in this world that I care about or even think about is getting out of this hellhole and coming home to you. Lila don't think I'm a big baby or coward because I'm not and if you could only see the many guys over here that feel the same as I do because there are a lot of them. And then there are some fools who have found a home in the Army and are even turning down being rotated out of here just to make an extra stripe or two. Darling don't ever worry about me doing a thing like that because making a rank doesn't mean that much to me, and I wouldn't stay if I were made a commissioned officer. So, honey, just remember that I'll leave here the very first chance I get, and I'll be going so fast that they won't be able to see me for the dust.

Well honey, there isn't anything of much importance that I can tell you about that's going on over here because things haven't changed any since the last letter I wrote you, in which I talked about and covered everything well as to what I am doing. Right now, in fact for the past week, we have been doing very little shooting and things seem to be pretty much at a stand-still. Except, of course, the Infantry outfits are still fighting probably as much as always. I guess they never get a rest, and I can well imagine what they are going through because we have it plenty rough and they always get a worse deal on everything, so I should be thankful that I got as good a deal as I did. If it wasn't for the terrible living conditions and the filth, things wouldn't be so bad. No kidding honey, it is impossible to keep clean. It seems like the more you wash the more you must, but I am getting used to sleeping in dirt and filth that it really doesn't bother me anymore. Honey, by the time I get home again you will probably have to give me a few lessons on cleanliness because I am used to living like a pig.

Well Lila, it looks as though I might be taken out of the gun section and given another job because my right eardrum has become injured permanently. I can still hear well but I get a terrific pain in that ear every time the gun is fired, and it's been getting so bad lately that I can hardly stand it. Maybe I will be given a better job and I do hope so because I don't care for the guns too much anyway and they are dangerous to operate.

Well honey I must go on guard duty tonight, so I won't be able to say much more for now. You mentioned in one of your letters that you were going to send some pictures and I sure hope they soon get here. Honey, I know I would feel so much better to have some more pictures of you, for that is all in the world I have to remind me of you and home, and I will appreciate them very much. Darling, I hope everything is going alright with you and I hope you are enjoying the wonderful summer weather in Salt Lake. How I wish I were there to spend it with you, but maybe next summer I'll be home – let's hope that I am.

Honey, I do appreciate you writing, and I hope you will continue as often as possible because your letters do mean so much to me. I'll close for now but will write again soon.

With best wishes and all my love to you honey.
Your beat-up soldier,
Med

July 11, 1951

North Korea

My Dearest Lila –

Well honey, I still don't have much time as usual, but I'll try and write a few lines before bedtime and believe me I am sleepy because I was up all last night and have been going like mad all day. You know Lila, in my last letter I told you I might be given another job, due to my one ear bothering me, and it got so bad that I couldn't stand being around the guns at all. Well honey, I have another job, at least for the time being, and guess what it is? Battery Clerk! How and why they ever picked me for the job I'll never know because I've never had any experience whatsoever in that line of work, except of course, I do know how to type, and I have almost forgotten how to do that.

I must handle all the paper and book work in the Battery, type out all reports, keep a roster of every man and what his particular job is (approximately 150 men in the Battery). Also, I have been acting as mail clerk lately, so you see what I have had to put up with in the past few days. The old clerk was injured and sent to the hospital so he can't be of any help to me and nobody else around here knows a damn thing about clerking and they have turned the whole thing over to me. Honestly honey, I've been making a complete fool of myself. If someone knew the score and could help me until I become acquainted with things but, NO! Med must do it all himself. You know honey, I typed out a letter to the Commanding General yesterday and it was sent back to me three times before they would accept it and only because there were one or two little errors in the spacing. You couldn't hardly see them without a microscope.

Everything must be so-so, or it's rejected and done over, and I know I could handle the job if someone who knew would help me get started, but no such luck.

Darling, why don't you come over here and help me out? I'm sure that with your help we would get along fine. No kidding, I'm almost ready to tell them to go to hell and get somebody else, but I suppose I shouldn't say anything yet, for I may like the job once I get on to things. It does have its good points, as I am away from the guns (at least a few yards) and there is no manual labor attached. Also, I have my own jeep and driver to haul me around. Some deal huh? I suppose I have complained about enough for now, as you can see most of the letter is about my work, but I'm not going to let it get the best of me yet. As soon as the other clerk gets back from the hospital, he will probably take over again anyway.

The news today looks pretty good over here and I was told that the cease-fire treaty will go through. In a way, honey, I am tee-d off because if this war does end right away, I will have to stay here for a year's occupation duty plus the time I have already spent here, which makes me feel bad in a way because that only means that much longer I will be gone. I am so homesick and miss you so very much and it will be a shock to me if I must spend another year over here. There isn't any sense in crossing the bridge before I get there and maybe things will turn out for the best – let's hope. And darling, I hate to think of what I will look like if I must spend that much more time over here because I already look like a beat-up, haggard old man. Honey, I hope you won't disown me when I do get home as I have lost a great deal of hair and will probably be bald by the time I get to see you again. You know darling, we don't receive very good care over here and a person could go to hell in a hurry if he let himself go. I am trying to take the best care of myself possible under the conditions.

I received your pictures the other day and I was really glad to get them. Honey, I really get a kick out of them, especially the ones when you were at the beach. Gee honey, they really looked nice (sort of tantalizing you know) and how I wish I could have been there with you. Seeing the beach in the picture sure brings back memories as I would spend a great deal of time there when I was younger. Honey, I am so fat now that I would be ashamed to get in a pair of trunks. You really looked nice honey, and thanks for the pictures. Gerrie also looked like she was in a pretty good mood, and I hope she stays that way. The picture of Ken and Ralph was very good. It reminded me so much of the days I worked for Peyton. It was also good to see Walt in the picture as I don't have a picture of him either. Honey, the car looked good, what I could see of it, and I don't think you will ever have any trouble with it, as the '41 Chev is the best ever made.

The last letter I received from you, just two days ago,

I note what you said about Doug being home and I am really glad to hear he finally made it. I can well imagine how happy Gerrie must be and darling, the day I see you again – I'll feel the same way. Oh Lila, what a wonderful day that will be and I'm sure it will be the most memorable of my life. I love you very much Lila, and I hope time – will never change our feelings towards one another, because I know I will be gone a very long time and many things could happen during that time which would change things, but I'm hoping and praying it never will.

Darling, excuse me if I run off at the mouth in this letter because I am very tired and discouraged. I am really not myself lately, and I have so much on my mind that at times I don't give a damn what happens. Everyone has their moods and bad days and believe me, this is one of mine. My nerves have been on edge the past few days and I've had arguments with several of the fellows. I suppose I had better calm down or I will never get to leave this place.

I hope this letter will make sense to you, as my eyes have been closed most of the time and I'll admit – it's the worst letter I have ever written. Maybe I had better close for now and let's hope I feel better next time I write. Say hello to everyone for me. With all my love, to my best and only girl.

Your very lonesome soldier,
Med

P.S. Tell Doug hello for me. I sure wish I could be there to see him because I am sure we will never meet until this war is over and we're both home again. As you know Lila, he is my best friend and I do hope he will write before leaving.

Medford and my driver

Lila at the Great Salt Lake Beach

Front Line, North Korea

July 15, 1951

North Korea

Hello Dearest,

    Well darling, I received another of your ever-welcome letters today and was very happy as usual. You know honey, I'm receiving at least one letter from you every other day, so I think that is very good, don't you? Honey, I know I have said this before, but your letters mean more to me than anything in the world and I hardly know what I would do if I couldn't hear from you. Honestly Lila, I get so downhearted and discouraged that I just don't care what happens anymore and nothing seems important to me. Honey, I'm just living and that is all. At times I doubt very much if I can survive that long old road ahead. I just keep wondering, hoping and counting the long weary months which lie ahead, and I don't ever realize the time could go so terribly slow.

    I have been in Korea almost two months and I can truthfully say it's been like two long years. You know honey, it isn't easy to have to stay here and see all these guys going home on rotation. I'm not kidding when I say that some of them hardly know how to act because they are so overcome with joy and the idea of leaving here. Oh, how I envy them even though I know that my day will come sometime, but it's that everlasting waiting and wondering which I call a mental strain and honey, it really is. A soldier not only has to worry about the enemy, but he has mental discomforts as well. We were told in orientation, before we ever arrived in Korea, that a soldier has this trouble and I believe it now. Oh well, someday honey, I'll probably look back on all this and think of it as a worthwhile experience, but right now it's the worst thing I've ever been through.

At the present time all I think about is that wonderful day when I will leave here, and I've thought about it so much that I can picture in my mind just what I will do and how I will react. Anyway honey, it's something to look forward to. I love you so very much – it does give me an inspired and glorious feeling to know that I do have someone back home waiting for me and that does mean so very much to me. I'm sure that if some of these other guys, who don't care about home, had a sweet girlfriend such as you are waiting for them, I know they would reconsider and be as anxious to go home as I am.

Lila, please understand what I am trying to say, even though I can't concentrate and express to you what I mean, but I hope you don't get bored reading this letter, for I know I have complained and said the same thing every time I write you. But, darling, you may as well be known for it will probably show on my face and actions when you do see me. I do feel aged and something within me has changed – I probably won't know what it is until I return to civilian life again. Honey, please don't think I've changed towards you because I haven't and my feelings for you will remain the same always.

Lila, I do hope you are receiving my letters and from what I gather they must be awfully slow getting there. But darling, I do write as many and often as possible so believe me I'm sorry if you're not hearing from me. I'm getting along as usual, and things have calmed down considerably. I'm just keeping my fingers crossed in hopes that this cease-fire treaty will go through.

The last letter I wrote to you (I hope you received it) I told you of my new job and assignment. Well, I'm still working on it, and I believe everything will turn out O.K. I'm kept awfully busy as we have a great deal of out-going correspondence which I must type, but they don't rush me too much and I have ample time to get the work done. I only hope I can keep the job, for it is a pretty good deal. Guess what honey?

My name has been submitted for a promotion. So, I'll probably be a P.F.C. (Private First Class) before very long. I will then have one lonely stripe on my sleeve. It isn't much of a promotion, but everyone must start at the bottom.

In your letter today I note what you said about Doug and Gerrie taking you to a show and it was really nice of them honey. How very much I wish I could have been with you, but someday honey we will all have fun again and we do have a lot to make up for. I'm very glad to hear Doug is having a good time, and I can just imagine how very happy he and Gerrie must be. I'm hoping that he won't be sent to Korea, as I know very well how he will feel, and I do hope he is luckier than I have been. Honey, it seems as though I have lost all contact with Doug as the letters I wrote to him were returned with a "no record" stamped on them. Honey, if you can get his new address from Gerrie will you please send it to me? I would like to keep in touch with him.

Well Lila, I am very glad to hear that you are finally having summer weather there and I'll bet you're glad huh? I wish with all my heart we could spend the summer months together, for it is a beautiful time of the year and there is so much to do and see. I hope you are enjoying it honey, as much as possible, and just remember all the things we're going to do when I get home. Darling, take good care of that car, for I'm looking forward to that long ride we're going to take someday. Listen to me, I sound as though I were never coming home. Just ignore some of the things I say in these letters honey because I write so fast, I hardly know what I am saying. If the Army would only give me a little time maybe I could write a letter which is understandable.

My time has almost run out darling. I hope everything is O.K. with you and your folks. Lila, don't worry too much about me as I am getting along well except, you know how terribly homesick and lonesome I am. I love you honey, and my thoughts are ever of you and don't forget the many things we are going to do, for I have so much time to make up for with you.

Be good Lila and say hello to everyone. I'm looking forward to your next letter and I will try to answer as soon as I receive it.

With All my Love,

Med

Lila in front of Med's dad,
Henry Oliver Poulsen's chicken coop

July 22, 1951

North Korea

Hello Darling,

I received another of your sweet letters today and honey, and was very thrilled as usual, for as I have told you before – they are the only thing that keeps me going. I guess I needn't tell you again how cheap I feel for not writing to you more often honey, but really, I don't have the opportunity. I've told you all this before and I hope you understand what I mean.

My new job does keep me going and I don't think I have as much free time now as I did in the gun section. The work really isn't hard, but it does keep me going to keep up on all the correspondence and typing which must be done. You know Lila, I didn't ever think that the inside work of the Army was so complicated until I was given this new assignment as clerk. There are so many laws and articles under which every little thing must be done that I am in a complete fog as to what I should do. I do manage to get things done even if it does take a great deal of time. I'm hoping as time goes on that I will be able to pick things up and learn what the score is. If the old clerk gets back from the hospital, chances are he will teach me all I have to know pertaining to this work. If I were back in the states I would be required to go to a clerk-typist school which every clerk has to do, so you see why it's been so rough on me cause the only knowledge I had pertaining to this job is – that I could type.

Well honey, I told you in my last letter that I was going to be promoted to a P.F.C., and the promotion has already been granted so I am now Private First Class. Honey, I know you will probably write some letters between now and the time you receive this letter, but after you do get this, please, be sure to put P.F.C. in front of my name when you address it, instead of Pvt. If we don't do this, chances are it will run into some complications, and I may never receive my mail. More Army red-tape you know. Honey, if the folks haven't heard by the time you receive this will you please tell them the same thing? Darling, I want to make sure nothing happens to my mail because that is all I care about (especially yours).

Well, dearest, I suppose there isn't anything I can tell you about going on over here that I haven't already said in previous letters. We are occupying the same positions and have been for almost a month. Honey, we are still in a little town called Habang-Yung, North Korea. It isn't much of a place and you will probably never hear of it, but if you do remember that's where I am, at least for the time being. We are still waiting and hoping for the outcome of the cease-fire talks and everything seems to be at a stand-still. The last position we were in (about a month ago), known as Ndong-Ni, North Korea, is the one where we caught most of the hell. At that time, I was working on the guns and believe me, I will never forget it as we were firing on the Chinese day and night almost as fast as the guns could be loaded. Perhaps I am saying too much, but anyway Lila, I witnessed some memorable experiences there – some which I will always remember.

I guess you have heard about the numerous rains we are having over here, and I can say that I'm getting awfully tired of it. It isn't very pleasant to go around wet all the time and sleep on the damp ground, but maybe the rain will soon end – I hope so. You know darling, there are a lot of snakes and frogs over here and when it rains so heavy, they really stir around, so much so that they are even taking refuge in my tent. I can't say that I enjoy having a snake in bed with me which almost happened the other night. It wasn't quite dark, and I could see a snake curled up in the corner and believe me I didn't waste any time in getting rid of it (about two feet long) but it could have bitten me and may even have been poisonous.

Honey, I note what you say about the terrible floods in Kansas and Missouri. I have been reading about it too as we get a paper every now and then to read. Darling, I'm sure thankful that you don't live in Kansas because if you did, I would probably worry myself sick about your being safe. It's bad enough being apart the way we are now. Darling, I'm thinking of you constantly and all the good times we could be having together, but honey, I know all our hoping won't be in vain and we will do those things together. The time does seem to be going awfully slow, although I have been in Korea almost two months, so the time is passing by slow but sure.

    Lila, I hope you won't be ashamed to be seen with me as I will probably be a physical wreck. I guess age creeps up on everyone and over here a person can age really fast. I probably won't have any hair, any teeth, and may not be able to hear very well due to my right ear being hurt. So darling, if you can overlook all of this, I will feel very relieved. (Big joke huh?) I had better quit talking or my hair may fall out entirely.

    Lila, in your letter I note what you say about loaning Doug and Gerrie your car and I think it's real sweet of you. But like you said, I am sure they would have done the same for us. Do you know exactly where or what camp Doug will be stationed at? I sure wish I could have seen him, and I can well imagine how fast his ten days must have gone as I can remember very well the 19 days I had seemed like overnight. Darling I just didn't have enough time with you. I guess Gerrie is very lonely again huh? Honey, you said how lonely you and Gerrie were, but remember Doug and I are also very lonely so I guess we can all share in each other's miseries. That statement may sound a little far-fetched, but it's exactly the way I feel.

    Darling, you know before I left, I told Mrs. Peyton that I would drop her a card, but as you know I don't have much time. Will you tell the Peytons hello for me, and everything is O.K.? Not that they are too interested in me, but I thought I would tell you that in case you see them.

Well honey, the more I write the more I want to, but I must go on guard tonight atop a very large hill and it is very lonely as there are only two of us and the other guy doesn't talk much, so I had better get some sleep now if possible.

I hope everything is alright with you darling, as well as your family. Say hello to everyone and that I'm doing well under the conditions. I'll close for now and write again soon.

Loving and missing you always,
Med

July 26, 1951
South Korea

My Dearest Lila,

Well honey, I received a letter from you yesterday and was very thrilled as usual to hear from you again. Your letters are really coming thick and fast now, which makes me feel 100% better. Sometimes honey, I get one every day and when I know the mail truck is about due, I just can't wait until it gets here. Darling, you're keeping me posted well on all the news at home and I do appreciate it very much.

Honey, I noticed what you said about my ear and wanting to know if it is getting any better. Yes darling, it is much better. Since I have been away from the guns it has been getting much better and is almost well. My eardrum wasn't broken but has been weakened considerably although I can't tell too much difference in my hearing. I may not be able to hear quite as well but honey it really isn't serious so, please don't worry and I'm sure I will heal up completely with time. Darling, I love you more for wondering and worrying about me because it does make a guy feel good to know he has a wonderful girl back home who is wondering and waiting for his return. I am O.K. You know me, I've always been the pessimistic and moody type.

Lila, the other day our Battery moved back south, across the 38th Parallel and we are now in South Korea, near a city called Chungcheong. We will occupy what is known as a "Rest Area" and are approximately 45 miles from the front lines. Honey, there is no shooting going on whatsoever, and we are in no danger at all. They have a movie every night, a large river to go swimming in and we get beer rations quite often now. There is no need for worry at the present time as everything is going smooth, and the morale is very high among the boys. As to how long we will be here, I can't say and if the cease-fire talks fall through, we will go back to the front again and continue shooting up the land again as we did before. I'm hoping and praying more than ever that this thing will end.

Honey, I noticed what you said about a mix-up at the bank, and I'll bet they really had you going. Darling, that's exactly the way things have been going with me and my new clerk job. The Orderly room (tent) here, in which I work, is so confused and in such a complete turmoil that I feel as though I could tear all my hair out. (I hadn't better, it's all falling out anyway! Big joke!) But anyway honey, the first Sergeant is so absent-minded that all his mistakes reflect on me and then I catch hell. The Sgt. doesn't know anything and really should be helping me out, but the way things are now nobody knows anything. I'm not going to worry about it, I'll do my job the best I can and that is all. You know honey, at first, I'd almost forgotten how to type but now it's all coming back to me, and I don't have any trouble as far as typing is concerned. I've already told you all of this before and so you know by now what I am doing.

I received a letter from the folks yesterday. They told me you and Gerrie had been down to see them. Darling, they are always pleased when you visit them and said they think you and Gerrie are very nice girls, and that they like you very much. Honey, I love you very much, and someday maybe not too long from now I can tell you personally how much I love you and have missed you.

Lila, things are looking a little better over here but still, I hate Korea and I hate the Army, everything about it. The day can't come too fast when I'll be leaving here for good.

I received a very welcome letter from Doug the other day and I could easily tell his feelings for the Army are the same as mine. I can just imagine how he hated to leave Gerrie and go back to that dreaded hole. That's just what it is honey, but the conditions for the troops in the states are so much better than over here, but I'm getting used to it now. Well honey, we are still having lots of rain over here and it's getting rather tiresome being wet and having the ground so damp, but the rainy season will soon be over – I hope! Here's to hoping that everything is alright with you, honey. Take real good care of yourself. Say hello to everyone for me and I'll write again soon.

With all my Love,

Med

P.S. Remember to put Pfc. in front of my name.

Well, honey, we arrived [in] Yokohama last night at ? o'clock P.M. After being up all night without a wink of sleep we are finally getting situated [in] our new camp, which is located just 17 miles from [To]kyo. By the way, it is called Camp Drake. How far I know we will be he[re] [for] a short time — may [be] a day or so and after that I cannot say. Most of the me[n] have been going to Korea, [how]ever, I am putting every [ounce of] faith and trust in the L[ord] that I won't be sent there.

CHAPTER SEVEN

Entire 7th Division Ordered Back to Front Lines

"As I told you before, I wish I could
    kiss you every time I think of you
and Lila, that feeling grows more
    as time goes on."

August 4, 1951

North Korea

Hello Darling,

Well honey, it's been almost a week since I have written to you, so I guess I had better get on the ball and scribble out a few lines before chow time. I have been awfully busy again lately and haven't had much chance to write until now.

In the last letter which I wrote to you, I told you of our Battery moving to South Korea for a rest. Well, that didn't last very long as we are now in North Korea again on the "line". The rest sure seemed good, but it didn't last very long, which I expected. As you know, the cease-fire deal has almost fallen through, so it looks like we will be going at it again as strong as ever. There has been a report lately that the Chinese are massing more troops and equipment, so it looks as though they will start with another drive. We may launch a counterattack first which I hope because if we strike first they won't have a chance to get organized as they were before. The entire 7th Division has been ordered back to the "front lines" and that's why I am expecting another battle, for they have led most of the other pushes. Honey, I hate to tell you this but things are shaping up that way fast so you may as well know now if we should start fighting again. We are near the city of Cheorwon, Korea, so honey if you ever hear of it, you will know that I am there.

Honey I finally received your very nice package, which came yesterday. I was beginning to wonder whether it was going to get here, for I noticed you mentioned it several times in your letters, and it really did take a long time getting here. It did get here in good shape and darling, I want to thank you ever so much as it did please me very much. The candy was very good, and the cigarettes were just as fresh as they would be in the store. You are sweet honey and very thoughtful. As I told you before, I wish I could kiss you every time I think of you and Lila, that feeling grows more as time goes on.

Darling, I guess I am in one of those moods again because I have been thinking of you and home, and all the wonderful things that we could be doing together. I've thought so much that I hardly get any sleep at night, but I guess I will get over it – I always do. I do love you so very much Lila, and I'm counting on the day when I can tell you just how much you do mean to me. You know, honey, in a letter I think it is very hard to express one's feelings and emotions, but I hope you do understand what I am trying to say and my feelings toward you.

You know, dearest, I am now starting my third month in Korea. Really honey, when you think back, it doesn't seem like I have been here that long, at least it doesn't to me. Maybe the time will pass more rapidly after the third month. Everyone tells me that it does because I will then be on the latter part of my term instead of the first. Honey, I'm still counting on only six months here, so let's keep our fingers crossed and hope nothing happens to interfere with our plans.

Well Lila, this will have to be a very short letter, as I have some unexpected work to catch up on. I did want to write a few lines and let you know that everything is O.K. Darling, please don't worry about my ear, for it is healing fast and doesn't bother me but very little. Also, my new job is coming along much better and I'm not having too much difficulty. Be good honey, and don't worry. I'll write again soon.

With all my Love,

Med

Entire 7th Division Ordered Back to Front Lines

Headquarters Battery, Korea 1951
Picture taken for 8th Army Newspaper, Med on right

August 16, 1951

North Korea

Hello Darling,

Well dearest, I received two more of your very sweet letters today and was very happy as usual to hear from you. Honestly Lila, I can't begin to tell you just how very much they mean to me. I am so thrilled and relieved that I hardly know how to act. Darling, if I thought I couldn't ever hear from you again I'm sure that I would go crazy. That may sound a little funny but it's the truth and I'm just living for your letters because they are all that keep me going.

Darling, as I informed you in my last letter, we are back in North Korea again, but haven't been doing much of anything since our return over here. The situation seems to be pretty much in hand and still awfully quiet. As to what's going on and what might develop in the future I cannot say. One day we are told the war is almost over and then the next day they tell us to be on the alert for a big push by the Chinese, which will mean another big battle. So far, the cease-fire talks haven't accomplished a thing and is very doubtful if they will. But honey, I guess I shouldn't complain if things aren't any worse here than they are at the present time.

No kidding Lila, I'm getting so lazy I hate to even move around. The past few days I haven't done one thing but sleep and eat and I can truthfully say that

I would much rather be doing something. The time seems to drag by so slow and allows a person to do a lot of thinking – maybe too much. I've found that when my mind is occupied I do feel much better. Maybe I shouldn't be talking about nothing to do because if we do start fighting again everyone will be plenty busy – too busy. I shouldn't complain when I have things easy.

Honey, I suppose you have heard of the Army's new rotation plan which I think is a damn dirty deal. You know darling, how much I've hoped and counted on getting out of here when six months are up, but now everything has been changed. The present rotation plan has been done away with and now they have devised a new point system which will determine when an individual can come home. For six months in Korea, in a combat zone which I am in now, we will be credited with 24 points, but instead of going home as before, we will be sent to Japan or somewhere else in the Far-East to make up the remaining points before coming home. The total number of points required at the present time is 36. So, you see honey, I don't have any idea whatsoever when I'll see you again. There is a very good chance that I may be here for the remainder of my Army time, which will be over a year from now. Darling believe me, I don't enjoy telling you all this but you may as well know what's going on. Lila, I felt so damn bad when I heard all this that I hardly knew what to say and it isn't easy to have to tell myself that I'm going to be away from you that much longer. Every time I have planned on anything it has been sure to go wrong, so from now on honey, I'm going to let things run their course, for I know that my yearning and hoping isn't going to do any good.

Sometimes Lila, I don't care what they do with me. I know that isn't the proper attitude to take, but really honey, after so long of this torturesome life over here, it begins to show on a person and gives him that "don't care" attitude. However, there is some consolation which does help, and that's knowing that someday, sometime, I will be able to return home. How long it will be is anyone's guess and I will be much better off if I don't think about it too much.

Darling, I hope you understand what I mean and have been trying to say. I just can't help myself for feeling this way and I assure you that I'm not alone in my feelings, as there are many more fellows here who feel the same and have wonderful girlfriends (such as you) to return home to. As for the other guys, I feel sorry for some of them because they have no aim in life whatsoever, only the Army. That's all they care about.

Lila, I do love you so very much and I need you, maybe more than you think. That's why this whole rotten set-up seems so unfair. In my opinion, this will be two or more years of my life totally wasted and it's for sure I'm not getting any younger. Darling, it is expecting a lot for you to wait that long, but it does make me very happy to know you are. No kidding Lila, if it weren't for you,

I would probably feel the same as so many of the other guys and maybe even stay in the Army. But honey, there's no danger of that and the glorious day when I will come home can't get here too fast. Well, I'm talking in riddles again so maybe I should let this subject go for now.

It was very sweet of you to send me Doug's address honey but guess what? I lost it already. At the time I received your letter we were in the middle of the worst rainstorm yet. On top of this we had to move to a new position and during the confusion the letter was lost, in fact several of your letters. I've been trying to keep most of them, but it isn't easy to do when we are on the move so much. Honey, will you please send Doug's address again? This time I will make sure it doesn't get lost. I would like to write Doug a letter, as he probably wonders what happened to me.

I noticed in one of your letters what you said about the girls at the bank being so stupid, especially the one that used the corny date. Honey, that's exactly the way many of the guys here do their work. If you don't keep an eye on them, they will be sure to do everything exactly the opposite of what they should. Oh well, they probably think the same of me, so I had better shut up.

Honey, you mentioned that Gerrie showed you the letter which I had written to her. I don't mind at all, for I have never said anything or could say anything about you that I would be ashamed of. How could I, and darling you are everything to me that I said and even more.

Lila, I hope I didn't say anything that would shock you about marriage, for that's exactly how I feel, and I hope you do likewise.

Well, I guess there isn't much more to talk about except that we are still having some terrible rainstorms over here. No kidding, they are so fierce that it hurts to remain outside very long during a storm. I mean that the raindrops are so large and come down with such terrific force that it really packs a sting when they hit you. The night before last we had a storm which lasted ten hours without even slowing up. My tent was completely washed out, my bedding was soaked so I had to get out in the middle of the storm and pitch my tent again. After an hour or so of fighting the wind and rain I finally got it up but had to sit up all night because my clothes and bedding were drenched. Some fun huh? I'll never forget that night or many others as the same thing happened.

Well honey, I've got some typing to do so I will close for now. I'll try to write again soon.

With all my Love,

as always, Med

P.S. Tell everyone hello

August 26, 1951

North Korea

My Dearest Lila,

    I received several more of your ever welcome letters in the past few days honey, and as usual I feel so much better. I honestly don't know what I would do with myself if it wasn't for your letters coming as often as they do. It's the same routine around here every day. When I'm not working, all I do is sit around and look wise. There isn't any place to go or anything to do which at times is almost enough to drive a person crazy. Sometimes I almost wish I was on the guns for they do help to break the monotony and can be very exciting when the Chinese are making another push or counterattack. I'm sure though that my ear would never withstand the terrific concussion. Maybe I just don't realize that I do have a good deal. As far as work goes, it is by far the easiest job I have ever had and will probably take some time to become adjusted to it. I'm getting along alright with the job, and I can say that I have learned a great deal about the functioning and methods by which the Army carries on its correspondence and other operations.

    Well darling you told me so much news in your last letters and they all came at once, that I hardly know what to write about. Honey, if in my letters you notice that I don't answer or talk about the questions you ask, please don't think it isn't because I don't read them or don't care because I do very much. I read every little thing you tell me over and over. I'm very much concerned about the affairs back home and especially you, honey, but I find it difficult to write about everything you tell me as I'm not able to write nearly as often as I should like in answer to your letters. But darling, I do appreciate your telling me all the news and I feel very fortunate having a sweet girl like you keeping me posted on the conditions at home.

I read the clipping you sent about Mr. Peyton, and I was interested in it. He's still the same old Paul, very thoughtful and big-hearted. I imagine the Sea Scouts appreciate his donating the building which will make a nice resort for them. I'm glad he and Mrs. Peyton think about me once in a while as I have thought about them also. It does make a person feel good to know he is missed and has friends back home. Tell them hello and that everything is fairly well over here.

I noticed what you said about you and Gerrie having a good time with Walt, Tom and Bonnie. I'm glad that you did honey, and it makes me feel good to know that you did enjoy yourself. Darling, there isn't much sense in both of us sitting around so whenever you can go out, I wish you would. But I'm not forgetting all the time I've lost, and we (you and I) will have many wonderful times to make up for. Lila, remember every place you go I am there in thought and spirit, so try to enjoy yourself for both of us.

Darling, I've given up thinking about rotation as

it only makes my thoughts and emotions much more confused. I know for certain it will be a long time before I get home so I might as well quit thinking about it. I've been in the Army long enough to know how they can change things and go back on their word. In the meantime, I'll just have the make the best of it (conditions over here) which sometimes isn't easy to do.

You wanted to know how close we are to the front. Well honey, I would say approximately five miles, which is very close for the Artillery – too close. Our guns will reach 9 ½ miles, but we have always been much closer, within that range, to the front which could be and has been dangerous at times. I'm not too awfully far from the guns and occasionally I can still feel the effects of the shooting in my one ear. It is improving and I think will heal up entirely in time.

Lately there has been quite an amount of activity over here. The past few days the guns have been roaring day and night - almost continuous firing. It seemed like old times again after our long rest (big joke huh?) There has been some excitement, but it wouldn't do for me to tell about it. By the way, honey, we are still in the East-Central Front and still in the mountains. We are near one small town which is called Uppikkinae, Korea. Not very easy to pronounce is it?

Honey, I've run out of paper, but the idea of Walt sending a bottle does sound good – hope it will get here. Honey, I am just getting over a bad case of dysentery, probably caused by drinking some unpurified water which I didn't know about. I have been quite sick the past week and have hardly had anything to eat, but I do feel better now. It can make a person very ill and I'm glad I am over it.

Darling, I hope you have a good time if you go on the camping trip with Dick and Nellie. I'll be thinking of you and wishing very much I could be with you. I had better close for now but will write again soon. Be good honey and take good care of yourself.

With Everlasting Love,

As Always, Med

P.S. Tell your folks and Gerrie hello.

P.S.S. Yes, it still rains as hard and often as ever (almost every day).

September 4, 1951
North Korea

My Darling Lila,

Well honey, I have a little time to myself so thought I would write a few lines before they give me something else to do.

I do hope you are receiving the letters I have been writing lately. Honey, since I have taken over assistant mail clerk, besides my other job, I have learned that many of the letters are being sent to the States by ordinary mail instead of airmail, even though I do write air mail on them. So, Lila, if it ever seems as though my letters are taking a long time to reach you – you will know the reason why.

Darling, it's really getting to be quite a problem thinking of something to write about. Every time I do write it's always the same thing over and over. Honey, I hope my letters aren't too boring; they certainly must be.

I just now received another of your letters dated 27 July. Darling, I'm happy as always to hear from you, but it makes me feel badly to think you haven't heard from me in two weeks! I'll admit that I have been extra busy the last two weeks, but there are some letters on the way and should have been there by now. Just like I said, honey, they do travel awfully slow from Korea to the States. Not only my being busy, but the first Sergeant has been ill the past week, which gives me so much more work to do. However, honey, I have been writing at every opportunity possible.

Lila, I understand what you mean when you say you're anxious. I am the same way, but you do write so much more and of course, I don't have to wait so long between letters. Darling, I'm so very thankful that you do understand and don't mind waiting to hear from me.

Apparently other people don't seem to understand what I mean. It seems everyone has stopped writing to me for some reason or other. The folks still write quite often but as for others, I don't know. Honey, I really don't care too much for I know I still have your very sweet letters to look forward to and that's all that matters. Darling, believe me, if I had to depend on other people for the news and goings-on back home, I wouldn't know very much. Your letters mean everything in the world to me, nothing else matters. Darling, this may sound silly, but I do have a hard time trying to concentrate and express myself lately. Believe it or not, sometimes it has taken days to finish one letter. I think I have something interesting to say and write about, but when the time comes to put it on paper, my mind is a complete blank. It didn't seem to be that way at first – maybe I'm cracking or may even be a little mentally upset. I don't know. All in all, I think you know what I'm trying to say – and hope you will bear with me. Other people probably don't realize what's happening over here; they seem to think this is a big picnic or something. I'm not going to worry about it, if they don't want to write – that's their business. It makes me very happy to know that you haven't forgotten me, and I love and admire you even more for your thoughtfulness. I'll be ever so thankful for the day I can cast this letter writing business aside and tell you in person how I feel, and how much you mean to me. I love and miss you so terribly much Lila; I always will.

Honey, please don't worry too much about me as I'm getting along about the same and feel pretty good. I know it is the nature of every person to worry, especially under conditions such as these, and I wonder and worry about you also but when you stop and think, it doesn't do much good and things could be so much worse. Lila, if I sound depressed and moody in some of my letters, please don't take too seriously everything I say. As I have said before, I'm very pessimistic and always expect the worst to happen. I should be thankful that I'm not in the Infantry for they do have some almost unbearable conditions to face and undergo. Someday, when I think back and recall this most trying experience now, I'll realize just how much I did have over many of the other soldiers. Maybe I just don't recognize a good deal when I have one.

Darling, there isn't much to say about the happenings over here as they haven't changed much since my last letter. It is true they have started fighting again and our guns have been roaring constantly, day and night, but I'm getting really used to that now. There are other things I could tell you, but they really aren't important.

Honey, I'm very glad that you see my family as much as you do. They think an awful lot of you and appreciate your visits very much. That goes double for me honey, as there's no girl in my sight who compares with Lila. You're everything to me darling, and I love you for every little thing you do. Lila, you're on my mind so much, maybe that's why I can't think straight anymore. Honey, see what you do to me ~ But I love it, feeling just the way I do. I'm thinking always of the time we can be together, and what a wonderful day that will be. Probably the most memorable of my life.

Well darling, there isn't much more for me to say for now. The rainy season has finally stopped, which makes me very happy. The nights are getting cool, just as you said they are back home, which reminds me so much of autumn in Utah. Honey, this time of the year always reminds me of football, one of my favorite sports. If you get a chance to see a game, please enjoy it for me also.

You spoke of the new addition to your family, and I'm glad your sister had a boy. You wouldn't want the girls to over-rule the family, would you?

Well darling, I'll close for now and try to write again soon if my mind will only concentrate on one thing at a time. Say hello to my unforgettable friends if you see them.

Loving and missing you Always,

Med P.S.

Honey, our positions are still on the East-Central Front, and we were near the vicinity of Chorwon. But, the United Nations have advanced quite a distance forward, so our positions are still quite a distance from the front and reasonably safe.

15 September 1951

North Korea

Hello Honey,

Well darling, I hope you will forgive me for waiting so awfully long to write but honey, we've really been busy – and I do mean busy! In the past week we have moved to new positions twice, and that always makes extra work for everyone. Not only that but the new First Sergeant doesn't know too much about the work, so it gives me more work and responsibility. He seems to be a pretty good guy and it won't be long until he can take over. You know honey, the past few days I have been acting as First Sergeant while this guy learns more about it. Big wheel huh? (joke)

Anyway honey, I have learned a lot since I've been Battery Clerk and I'm beginning to like the work quite well. I realize now that I was fortunate in getting the job. The weather is getting cold now and I can see how miserable and discouraging it is for the men who work on the guns. They work in all kinds of weather, very little sleep, and the guns are quite dangerous to work with, especially when being fired continually as they get hot and could blow up, which has happened twice since I have been in Korea. Darling, I have never told you this before because I didn't want you to worry, but it was a mess (the guns blowing up) and I shall never forget it.

As I was saying, Lila, the weather is getting cold, but I don't think I will suffer too much, as we have ordered a stove for the tent which will help a great deal. The First Sergeant ordered the stove for us, so I'm quite certain we will get it as he has a lot of authority. Darling, I guess I'm lucky to be working with him for he does help me out and gets me most anything I need.

Darling, I received two more of your ever welcome letters in the past few days and I do appreciate every one of them. I only wish I could write as often as you do. I have waited longer this time through no fault of mine, but I'll try to do better in the future.

Honey, thanks a million for the cigars. Yes, I do smoke them especially since I have been in Korea. Maybe I shouldn't, but really there isn't much to do for enjoyment. If I don't inhale all the smoke, they shouldn't both me too much.

Darling, give my best regards to your sister and husband and thank Russ for the cigars. Congratulations for the new nephew – I'm glad he is a boy. Ha ha!

You mentioned something about the overnight trip you went on with Dick and Nellie. Honey, I'm glad you had a good time and hope you will continue to enjoy yourself as much as possible. Darling, I'm just like you in wishing we could have been together. Someday, maybe not too long from now, we will all take a trip together. Lila, I do love and miss you so very much, and that far-distant day when we will see each other can't get here too soon. But honey, I find that I feel better if I don't think too much about rotation. I've noticed that the time does pass more quickly when my mind is occupied, and I am not thinking too strongly about rotation. The day will come, and it is a wonderful feeling to know that as each day passes it brings me that much closer to coming home to you. Just think honey, it won't be long until we'll have five long months behind us.

You know Lila, the other day our Battery was honored by firing the 100,000th round or shell, since the Battalion of guns arrived in Korea one year ago. We all felt deeply honored (joke) as General Keifer himself fired the guns, more or less, for publicity. I guess we should feel proud as our Battery was chosen from four other Batteries to fire the round. The reason I am telling you this is because several pictures were taken of the ceremony and may be published in the States. I wasn't in the picture (almost) but if you see it, you'll know what the score is and that I belong to that organization. Darling, it was the gun I was assigned to before they transferred me to Battery Clerk that fired the round. Chances are if I were still in the gun section I would have been in the picture. I feel honored that our Battery was chosen for the occasion. Each shell costs $100, so you can see how much money it is costing the United States to remain in this stupid war, as our Battalion (4 Batteries) have fired 100,000 shells in one year. That's a lot of money to shoot away with just 24 guns, don't you think? Well darling, I hope you can make sense out of all of this. It was something to talk about.

I don't have much time left so I will close for now. Darling don't worry too much as I'm getting along O.K. and feeling pretty good. I hope everything is alright with you and your family. I hope you're getting along O.K. at the bank. Honey don't let them work you too hard because I want you in top condition when I get home, as we will have so many things to do. Say hello to everyone. I'll write again soon.

With Everlasting Love,

Med

P.S. Honey, thanks again for sending me Doug's address. I wrote him a letter last week. Hope he receives it.

September 21, 1951

North Korea

Hello Honey,

I received another of your letters today and honey I was as happy as ever to hear from you. Your letters seem to be getting here without too much delay and I'm thankful for that. As I have said before I don't know what would happen if I couldn't hear from you as often as I do.

From the way you talked the bank must really be going full force. Honey, ten hours a day is too much, even for a man to work. I hope that doesn't happen very often. Darling, I don't want them to overwork you and they certainly must be. You give them the word, won't you? Maybe you feel as I do. Working does pass the time away but there is also a limit to everything. Well anyway honey, you take it easy and don't over-do yourself! Darling, I'm always wondering how things are going with you, and I do hope everything is under control.

I can't think of anything new or exciting to tell you of happenings over here. The conditions remain the same as they were in my last letter. However, the Infantry has its frequent clashes with the enemy, which doesn't affect us too much; only when either side decides to make a drive, then we (the Artillery) are called upon to render our support. Sometimes though our guns fire continually for hours in such an assault, but I'm getting used to the noise, which is a common occurrence. Lately the Chinese have made another futile attempt to push our forward positions back, but always end up being driven back themselves. Honey, I don't think we need to worry about conditions as they seem to be pretty much in hand.

Darling, in some of my letters I may sound discouraged and depressed but don't take too seriously the things I might say. I have always been one for jumping to conclusions before there is any need so try to overlook some of my statements – they probably are exaggerated to a certain extent. Human nature you know. I've been thinking how fortunate I was to be assigned to the outfit I'm with instead of Infantry or the Marines, and various other units which aren't any better. They really do experience some almost unbearable hardships and are exposed to the worst of weather conditions. It is true that I will be here this winter but will at least have stoves and I'm sure they don't have stoves in their fox holes to keep them warm. Darling, I am thankful for my job and everything else I have achieved through blessings of the Lord even though I don't deserve it. There are many temptations in life, which I think are a test in the view of the Lord to determine just how strong we really are. I'll admit I have been weak in many things, but I am trying to do the best I can which I know isn't good enough. Honey, I feel that my blessings have been granted through the prayers of someone else, more than my own. Yours and my wonderful parents I think, have been far more influencing than the prayers which I have offered. Anyway honey, I am very grateful, and I realize more and more that I have been blessed. Lila, I only hope that someday I will lead a better life than I have done in the past. Darling, you probably are wondering why I am telling you all this, but they are my true feelings and something to talk about. Being so far away and in conditions such as these seems to give a person a clearer understand and realization of what life is all about.

 Well darling I wasted most of my time jabbering but

I did want to write this letter today, for tomorrow we may move to a new location, and I would be busy for a few days not being able to write.

Honey, you spoke about having a cold and I hope you soon get over it. I know how miserable they can make you feel, so take care of it. I hope everything is O.K. with your family. Say hello to them. Above all Lila, don't let them work you too hard at the bank!

Don't worry about me, lover. I'm getting along alright and I'm feeling better as time goes on to know that I will soon have four months of my time in Korea. Maybe if I continue being blessed, I can get out of here sometime this winter. Let's hope!

Well honey, I'll close for now. Be good and take care of my girl for me!

With All my Love,

Med

P.S. Honey. I note what you said about Miss Utah winning the Miss America title. We get several issues of newspapers over here and in one of them it talked all about her being the new Queen. Honey, I'm proud too and I don't hesitate in telling the guys which state I am from. Ha!

October 2, 1951

North Korea

Hello Darling,

Well honey, in the past few days I have received several more of your very sweet letters and I still feel as badly as always that I can't supply you with as many letters as you do me. Darling, it's been a week or more now since I wrote the last letter, and the very thing came true which I expected – we moved to a new location the following day, which always brings on more work and confusion for everyone, until we at least get settled and can resume our normal operations. Right now, everything is under control, giving me the usual amount of leisure time to write or anything else I might want to do.

October 3, 1951

Well honey, I guess I spoke too soon! Last night right after I made the above statement, some unexpected work came in which kept me busy the remainder of the evening and all last night and today. I'm going to finish this letter tonight if it's the last thing I do! We are going to move (march order) again within the next two days, so I won't be able to write again for a few days. Darling, I'm really getting sick and tired of moving so often. We no sooner get settled in one place, then we move again. I'm guessing we have moved fifty or more times since my arrival in

Korea. I hate to complain but it really does get tiresome.

I don't know what to say about the conditions over here. Everything is pretty much the same except we have advanced deeper into North Korea territory. I think the Communists have fallen back some, so that sounds good. Honey, I think our next move will be back in the rear area; I am glad for that. Another rest will do us some good.

Darling, in one of your letters I noticed what you said about sending something for my birthday. Lila, it's very sweet and thoughtful of you but it brings on a problem for me, as well as you and mom. I've thought honey but I just don't have any suggestions at all. I have all the clothing I need, maybe more! I get all the cigarettes, candy and toilet articles I can use. I'm really eating too much candy, more than I have ever done before. But then again, darling, I guess we must eat something. Lila, I'm going to leave it up to you to decide if you really want to send something. We don't have much room to carry things and if I were to get something valuable it might get broken, which has been the case several times with other fellows. Darling, you understand, don't you? It is very sweet of you to remember. By the way we were told that any packages mailed to the boys over here should be sent between October 15 and November 1. This is largely due to the Christmas rush. So, lover, I'm going to let you decide.

Darling, I remember that you also have a birthday in November! I don't have much access to gifts over here, but I'm going to give mom the word. She or Nellie will have to help me out. Honey, there is something else we will have to celebrate when I get home. Both having birthdays in the same month!!

I received a letter from Doug the other day and was pleased to hear from him. It's been so long that I was beginning to wonder what happened to him. His letter was very nice, and I appreciate his writing – I'm going to answer it as soon as possible.

I imagine Gerrie is very excited about going to see Doug huh? I can well imagine how they both must feel. Lila darling, just imagine if that were you and I seeing each other! Honestly, honey, imagine how happy I would be. But I'm not forgetting that our time is drawing nearer each day and will soon come to pass. It makes me very happy and I'm living and fighting for that day – that day only. Darling, believe me when I say it will take more than the Army to keep us apart!

I'm glad to hear that your job is going alright, and everything is under control at the new Branch. I'll bet it's really nice. Honey, I'm proud of you for being on television. I wish I could see it. Well precious, I'll have to close for now. I'm very tired and my eyes are beginning to hurt. I've probably been straining them lately. Honey don't worry, I'm alright! Say hello to everyone and you be a good kid. I'll write again real soon.

With loads of love to you honey — Med

P.S. How is the car running?

October 15, 1951

North Korea

Hello Darling,

Well, honey, the excitement is all over! I've been extremely busy the past few days making out casualty reports and trying to get conditions in a normal status again. Darling, please don't get alarmed, as everything has calmed down now. I'm not going into detail as to what happened; I don't want you to worry. However, the 13th of October was an unlucky day. Our entire Battalion was hit by enemy artillery fire, but the casualties were considerably light. I was beginning to wonder how lucky we could be, for we moved right up on the front lines. To me, it was obvious that we would get it sooner or later. Darling, please don't worry about me; I was in a pretty safe place! There was a lot of excitement and confusion – breaks the monotony you know. I'm sure it won't happen again; at least I hope not!! We were all scared and learned how to take care of ourselves if the situation should repeat itself.

Darling, I received more of your ever-welcome letters the past week and I'm very sorry that I couldn't answer before now. In the first place we were all very busy and secondly, the entire Battery has been in a complete state of confusion and shock. You do understand don't you honey? Please try!

I note what you said about Gerrie leaving and I don't

blame her for being happy. I too would be happy if I could come and see you. Darling, I can understand what you mean about being lonelier now than ever. But Lila, I feel the same way and have ever since I left you. The days are passing by, one by one, and before long honey I will be home. The end of this month will make 5 months in Korea. Maybe after spending the winter here, I can come home. I'm counting on it very much and they hadn't better disappoint me. What do you think?

Rotation seems to be going along alright. Most of the old men are going or gone, which makes me feel much better, as that will make my turn that much closer. The point system has stopped again, through some unknown formality of the Army as usual, and I only hope they don't cheat me out of any points when it starts again. Each and every point will mean a great deal. Darling, just think, as of the 28th of next month, I will have one year of my Army life completed! I only hope that the next year will go by more quickly.

Darling, how is the job going? I hope you're not being worked too hard. You take it easy and give them the word.

How is the car running? I'll bet you're really a good driver now huh? Darling, you always did handle my car very nicely and I'll bet you are even doing better now, with more experience. Honey, you will probably have to teach me how to drive when I get home, as I've almost forgotten; it's been so long. The only practice I get is on a Jeep and not too much at that.

Entire 7th Division Ordered Back to Front Lines

Supply truck destroyed by enemy mine — one killed — Korea 1951

I imagine it's getting pretty cool there by now, isn't it? It sure is here, and the dreaded wintertime is on its way.

Darling, how is Utah doing in football this year? Are they getting beat as usual?

Well Lila, it seems as though I can't have any free time lately. I must get the mail for the Battery, so will have to close. Darling, I hope you receive what letters I do write. Please don't worry, I am O.K. and honey, I'm still thinking of you and loving you more than ever. Sometimes I wonder how I can hardly wait to get home and see you again. Darling, you've been with me every single minute since we were last together, and it is a wonderful feeling to know that I have such a sweet girl as you, who will be there when I get home.

Take it easy, darling, and say hello to everyone for me. How are the Peytons getting along, and your parents?

I'll write again as soon as possible.

With everlasting Love,

Med

---

24 Oct 51

North Korea

Hello My Dearest,

Well darling, I have covered a lot of territory since I last wrote to you. We have moved to the eastern "front", and it required two days traveling to get here. Sometimes I wonder how the Army operates. We had been moving around a great deal in the east-central sector, and then all at once they tell us we are going to the east coast and relieve part of the Second Division Artillery outfit. I'm glad we finally got here and are settled down for the time being at least. During that trip I got a pretty good idea of what the winter will be like over here, as I almost froze traveling all night, and I had plenty of clothes on or at least I thought so. We are now much higher in the mountains and believe me, it is cold! I only hope I can survive the winter without too much trouble.

Darling, I remember you asking in one of your letters just what Division I am with. I am assigned to the 7th Division Artillery and in my opinion it's a real sharp outfit. Not just because I am in it, but they have always had a good name and when any other outfit runs into trouble, the 7th is sent to relieve them, such as we are doing now.

Well honey, in the past week I have received several more of your ever-welcome letters and how very much I wish I could answer each of them without waiting so long. Lila, I try to let you know as often as possible that I'm O.K. and not to worry about me.

Darling, I also received the birthday present and card. Honey, I just can't explain to you how I felt when I read the beautiful verse on the card. The card itself was very beautiful, but darling – that verse! I'll bet I read it a hundred times and I'm still reading it. I don't know why, but it almost made the tears come to my eyes. Darling, maybe it's just knowing that it came from you, and my wishes were stronger than ever of coming home to you. Lila, as for the gloves, you really hit the nail on the head! You couldn't have given me anything more useful and appreciated. If I told you how cold it was riding in the open truck, and without the gloves I would have been miserable. We haven't been issued gloves as yet, and it may be some time until we are, so darling you couldn't have made a better guess! Thanks a lot honey; I do appreciate your thoughtfulness so much. I could probably use up all the paper in Korea trying to express my thanks and feelings, but dearest, I do hope you understand what I mean, and I'm waiting for the day I can tell you in person just how much I have loved you and missed you, and how much I have appreciated what you have done for me.

Darling, I told you that I mentioned to the folks about your having a birthday in November too. I wish I was there to take care of it myself, but under the circumstances I guess I can't make it (big joke huh?). Anyway darling, in case this letter is delayed I want to wish you now A VERY HAPPY BIRTHDAY, and all the luck and happiness that could come to anyone. And Lila, I do mean every word of it, with all sincerity, for honey, to me you are tops, and I love you very much. Nothing could be too good for "my girl" nor ever will be. Anyway honey, if you feel as I do our birthdays won't be enjoyed nearly as much as possible until we can spend them together. Just think, 23 years old and I do feel it! How about you? I will probably look 33 by the time I leave this "hell hole".

I'm very sorry to hear of you having troubles with the car. Maybe it's because I asked about it. I wish I were there to help you out, even though I don't know much about a car. I hope it's running alright now, and darling, do be careful.

Well, I have almost run out of time and haven't

begun to answer all your questions and talk about the things you do. I forget many of the things you ask me, but I do read each letter carefully, and enjoy hearing the news.

Have you heard from Gerrie and Doug? I'll bet they're really happy being together. Say hello to them for me.

Honey, my name has been submitted for another promotion. The orders haven't come back yet but when they do, I will be a corporal (two stripes). The stripes don't mean too much to me, but the raise in pay does. I'll let you know when the promotion goes through.

Well, Lila, it's very late so I had better close for now.

Floyd (Lila's dad), Lila, and
Eliza Irene Hansen (Lila's mother)

Say hello to your folks and any of my friends if you should see them. I'm going to write the folks a few lines tonight and thank them for the card also. Be good honey and take care of yourself.

Loving you Always,

Med

November 5, 1951

North Korea

Hello Darling,

Well Lila, it's been almost two weeks since I received your last letter, and I haven't been able to write before now. I'm very sorry darling, but please try to understand. So much has happened! Lately I have been so confused that I don't know which end my head is on.

To begin with, we have a new commanding officer, and he really is a _____??? _____!!! You know what I mean! He seems to enjoy working the men 24 hours a day without any rest. The past few nights I have been up until 3:00 in the morning typing out some of his nonsense, and then during the days I'm going as fast as I can. Someday, I'll see him when I'm out of the Army and ---well you can guess what will happen! Honestly honey, I can't even begin to tell you the confusion and inconvenience he has caused.

Not only that but we have also had more excitement, such as I mentioned before only not as bad. My tent was hit and burned to the ground (I'm sure glad I wasn't in it), including all my personal belongings. But being as it was, an emergency, my clothing will be replaced. Some of it has already. Darling, I'm not telling you all this just to give you something to worry about – not at all – it's just that I'm trying to let you know a few of the things that are happening over here, and it is something to talk about. Lila honey, please don't worry now as everything is under control once again, and I'm O.K.

Darling, I received the package you sent and couldn't even thank you until now. You're very thoughtful honey and I appreciate it so much. The candy and cigarettes are always welcomed and help when I run short. However, most of the time we get enough, at least we have them here. Lila, I guess there isn't any use in me trying to express my thanks for the things you have done because I just can't! I'm getting so I can't even think right anymore. Honey, I'm just waiting for the day I can come home and talk to you the way I want to. When that day will come is anybody's guess, but it is getting nearer.

I am now in my sixth month in Korea. Sounds pretty good, doesn't it? I'm certain that I will spend the winter here, but my hopes are very high of getting out of here sometime in the spring – maybe! I'm not going to count on it, as I've been in the Army long enough to know better.

Aftermath of my tent being hit by enemy fire

Darling, I spoke of a promotion in my last letter. Well, it came through and I am now a Corporal (two stripes). I don't care much about the rating, but the extra money will help. I'm surprised that I even got the promotion with this new joker in command.

Well honey, how is the job going? I hope they aren't working you too hard. They hadn't better be or I'll have to tell them off! The weather here is getting very cold.

LOVE LETTERS FROM HEARTBREAK RIDGE

NEAR MISS - CHINESE SHELL STRUCK NEAR MY TENT

TENT WAS DESTROYED

HEART BREAK RIDGE

M/SGT. EGGERT - KOREA - NOV. 1951

I hope that it will be a milder winter than last. Honey, we are in the area of the "Heartbreak Ridge." You've probably heard of it as it's been the center of attraction for quite some time. Well honey, there is no rest for the wicked. I've just been informed of some more work for me. I hope you're getting along alright. Darling, take care of yourself for me. Have you heard from Doug and Gerrie lately? Say hello to your folks and everyone else.

With all my love, darling – Med

P.S. Don't worry and be sure to put Cpl. In front of my name instead of P.F.C.

November 18, 1951

North Korea

My Dearest Lila,

Hello honey! How's the girl today? I hope you're getting along alright and not working too hard.

Darling, I have received two more of your most welcome letters in the past week. It's almost impossible for me to remember everything that is said, or asked, because sometimes it's a week or more before I can answer. But anyways honey, I never overlook one single thing you ask or say, so please don't think I'm neglecting to read them. I know you don't honey, but I'm just letting you know. Your letters mean so very much to me, and

I'll read every one of them no matter how busy I am.

Darling, forgive me if I'm wrong but yesterday was your birthday, wasn't it? Honey, I remember we were talking about birthdays once, and I tried to remember. Please tell me if I'm wrong. Lila, I wanted very much to write you yesterday, but it was one of those busy days and I only had time for the Army as usual. Anyway darling, I want to wish you a Happy Birthday – as happy as could be. Mine wasn't very enjoyable, that's why I wanted you to celebrate both. Honey, I'm not feeling sorry for myself, just hoping that I can be home with you when another birthday rolls around. It would be nice, wouldn't it, celebrating two birthdays in the same month? Someday it will be darling. Soon, I hope!

I gave mom the word, so hope she took care of the occasion for me. It is a crude way of doing things but since I'm not there I haven't any choice. I hope she gives you something that will be of use.

Well Lila, there isn't anything important to talk about as to the war situation. You probably know more than I do. As far as I'm concerned, the peace-talks can go to hell. They've tossed it around so much that I doubt very much if they will ever reach an agreement. Maybe I shouldn't talk that way, but it does get discouraging.

Lila, I'm well in my sixth month in Korea, which makes me feel a little better, even though the old men that have gone were here for nine to twelve months. The point system was stopped as of 31 August, and I only

Replacement tent — an upgrade!

had 13 points at that time. Unless they change that cut-off date, or recompute the points to the present date, I'll never get out of here. But honey, all the old men have gone so they should start on us soon, and the point system will have to be brought up to date. Let's hope, kid – maybe sometime this winter! They hadn't better let me down, or I'm liable to do something drastic.

Lila, I told you about the fire – well most of my clothes have been replaced. I'm in a big tent with a stove and cot so please don't worry about me honey. I'm O.K.

Well, how did the hunting season turn out? Did everyone get a deer and their limits of pheasants this year? I like to hunt them both and I missed it this year. But not the way I miss you, Lila!

I've been thinking all day how nice it would be if we

were together now. I love you very much my darling, and the love has grown deeper since I left you. I'll be so very happy when I see you again – happy that I could get through this mess and come back to you.

Well honey, it's almost chow time so I'll have to close for now. I'm glad that Gerrie is coming home. You'll be anxious to see her I know. Say hello to your folks darling and don't worry too much about me. I'll write again soon. A Happy Birthday again, honey!

With all my Love,

Med

---

2 December 1951

North Korea

Hello Honey,

Well darling it's only me again. I've been trying to write a letter to you for the past three days and I finally succeeded. It seems like every time I take a few minutes to write a letter some damn detail or unexpected job comes up. Only yesterday I started a letter and was interrupted before being able to finish. Honey, I'm going to finish this one if it takes all night, and they hadn't better bother me!

Darling, I received five more of your ever-inspiring letters the past week and was happy as always to get them. Honey, I wish I could write that often to you, but conditions won't permit. Lila, I know you understand, and I'm getting along alright; there isn't any need to worry.

Lila I'm glad you had an enjoyable Thanksgiving – as enjoyable as could be anyway. It's true that we had a very good dinner, considering Army cooks, but still I felt awfully lonely and homesick. I was wishing all day that I could have been home with you and the family. All I can do is hope and pray that by the time another thanksgiving rolls around I can be home to stay. So far, I have spent a birthday and thanksgiving here. Wonder what I'll feel like by the time Christmas gets here? I hate to even think about it. I know for sure though darling that you'll be on my mind even more than ever. But honey, it's nice just to think about you and no one, not even the Army, can ever stop me from doing that!

Lila, I'm glad to hear that you liked the birthday gift. Honey, it isn't at all the way I wanted it to be, but under the circumstances I had no other choice. Mom has always been pretty good at picking out gifts, so I thought it best to let her do it. I hope you liked it honey and I also hope you had a very happy birthday.

Darling, it sounds as though you are really doing alright in your ceramics class. I imagine it would be quite interesting and a very good pass time. I'll bet you are really getting to be quite an expert at it!

I received your clippings on the football situation,

and I must admit that I was surprised to see Utah at the head of the league. Usually, they don't have much of a football team, but I am very glad, and proud that they finished out first this year. I was reading in one of the papers we receive over here that they may get a chance to play in one of the bowl games. I sure hope so, and it would be an honor for all the players. Wish I was one of them. Ha!

Well Lila the situation over here hasn't changed any since my last letter. We are still in the same place and probably will be all winter. The fighting is still going on as usual. One night last week our Battalion of guns, and one Infantry Regiment killed 1,500 Chinese in a one-night assault. Quite a few huh? It seems to me that the damn fools would give up before we kill all of them!

Darling, I've quit thinking about the peace talks as they don't seem to get anywhere. There's no point in counting on them too strongly because they have fallen thru so many times that it could easily happen again. Maybe I'm talking crazy again, but it is discouraging.

Darling, I'm starting with my seventh month in Korea, and I don't see how they can possibly keep me here too much longer. But then I know the Army too; they can easily spoil a person's plans. Let's just hope darling that they will send me home sometime this winter.

I'm glad to hear that Doug and Gerrie are getting along O.K. I imagine they are very happy being able to see each other as often as they do. I hope Doug isn't shipped overseas. I know very well how he would feel.

Well dearest, it's getting very late and will soon be time to go on guard. I'm very happy that I was able to finish this letter tonight. Please don't worry too much darling, I am alright, and the time is nearing when we will see each other again. Oh, what a glorious day!

Be good honey and take real good care of Lila for me. Say hello to everyone –

Loving and missing you always,

Med

---

14 December 1951

North Korea

Hello Darling:

Well honey, after another week slipping by, I guess it's time I wrote a letter. Lila, I started a letter to you the day before yesterday but was interrupted, as usual, and could not finish. If there is anything that tees me off, it is starting a letter and not being able to finish! Especially to you darling! But anyway, I'm going to finish this one even if it takes all night.

Lila, I received another letter from you today. I'm always thrilled to get your letters honey; they mean everything to me. The mail situation is getting very slow as far as the letters are concerned, probably because of the Christmas rush. Sometimes it takes a week or more between letters, but when they do get here it's usually two or three at once. Darling, in your letter today I noticed you asked me to forgive you for missing a day or two without writing. Lila, you have been very faithful about writing me, and I'm sure that there isn't one single soldier in Korea who has received more letters from his girl than I have. I can truthfully say that it's been your letters that have kept me going when I've been in one of those frequent moods. No honey, I'm not forgiving you for anything because you've been very sweet about writing to me and I only wish I that I could write you as often.

Darling, I also received the Christmas package you sent to me, which arrived in very good shape. It's surprising that a package can travel thousands of miles without being damaged at all. I'm very glad though that they at least handle our mail with care. The chocolates were fresh and tasty. You know honey, that's the first box of chocolates I've seen in Korea! But then that's to be expected. I'll admit that the candy and pretty wrappings did make me homesick, but that's the way I like to feel. It seems more like Christmas anyway. We've been a little short on cigarette rations lately, so the carton of Lucky's could not have come at a better time. Thanks a million darling, you're very thoughtful. You've been nice and sweet to me honey. I appreciate it so much. Darling, if only you could wrap yourself up in a package and be shipped to me – what a Christmas present that would be, huh!! At the present time it's just wishful thinking but the time is nearing when it will come to pass. Darling, it can't be soon enough, for I love you so much and I've missed you more than I could ever miss anyone. At times, honey, I've thought you were beside me. That's how much I have thought of you! It hasn't been too awfully bad over here for that reason, but I'd hate to go through all these long months again because I know that it just can't be too long before we will see each other again!

Honey, I had to give mom the word again about Christmas. It isn't at all the way I wanted it to be, but I guess I have no other choice. I would like nothing better than to get you something myself, but I'm not at liberty to do anything. Lila, you know what I mean don't you? I hope she gets something that will be useful to you, honey.

> *The Red Cross supplied us with these cards, honey. Not too nice, but will have to do.*
>
> **Merry Christmas** and best wishes for the **NEW YEAR**
>
> *It doesn't say what I would like to say to you, darling, but I do wish you a very, very merry X'mas, and best wishes for my girl! And your family!*
>
> *With all my love, Sincerely darling, Ned*
>
> **KOREA 1951**

The situation over here is about the same as last time, except that there has been considerably more excitement. Today I witnessed one of the most horrible accidents that has occurred since my arrival in Korea. An Army Air Force plane crashed and it's two occupants were mutilated and burned beyond recognition. It's too horrible to talk about but a person doesn't get over a thing like that in just a few hours. I've seen many other incidents that were bad, but nothing like this. I guess such things are to be expected in war, and I'll probably see many more before leaving here.

Darling, lately I have been up on the front lines twice with the Infantry. It was really exciting – more than expected – and also a very good experience. I have been there several times before observing our firing on the enemy, and it's been very effective. It seems to me that the damn "Chinks" would quit!

I'm being well take care of darling so please don't worry too much. I hope you are getting along alright. Don't work too hard and take it easy! I'm glad that the bank officials have everything settled now.

Honey, is your mother home yet? Say hello to your folks for me. Merry Xmas again darling and I hope you can enjoy it for both of us. I'll write again soon.

With all my love,

Med

Entire 7th Division Ordered Back to Front Lines

Soldiers anxiously gather to receive their mail

21 December 1951

North Korea

My Dearest Lila:

How are things going honey? I hope everything is O.K. and are getting along as usual.

Darling, in the past week I have received two more of your very sweet letters. The last one came today. Honey, in the last letter I noticed that it had been quite some time since you had heard from me. I'm sorry darling, but the letters just don't seem to be getting through as quickly as they were two months ago. It tees me off to think that the Army can't provide a better mail system than they do. But I guess the delay is mainly because of the Christmas rush.

Lila, there are at least two more letters on the way besides this one and I hope you receive them before too awfully long. But darling, please don't worry because I'm getting along alright. I'm getting very homesick to see you and the family, and growing very tired of this way of life, but it doesn't do a bit of good to wish and complain. I've given up hope of getting out of here before a year's time is spent at least! Darling, I know all of this sounds crazy because I said in one of my last letters that I would stand a good chance of getting out of here this winter, but right now it seems all in vain because we're not getting any replacements and rotation has stopped! I've reached a point that I don't care anymore. Believe me Lila, I do want to come home to you – more than anything in the world but it's beginning to get a little tiresome and discouraging sitting here day after day wishing and hoping that it won't be too much longer. I'd honestly feel better if I were back in the states someplace in prison. I'm sure that I would have a better life!

Lately I haven't cared about anything, so I volunteered to go up on the front lines again as a member of an observing party for our guns. It's a good experience and very exciting plus it gets me out of the mood I'm in. The Chinks spotted us yesterday and tried in vain to get us out of there, but we were well "dug in". It takes something like that to make me appreciate how much life really means to a person, even though he is downhearted and depressed at the time.

I do have so very much to come home to, and I will if it takes ten years! I love you very much Lila, and I'm thinking of you more every day.

Darling, please don't think I'm strange and different when you see me. Maybe it's all in my head, but I feel as though I'm cracking up. I'm getting very absent minded and undependable. Maybe a rest will snap me out of it. I hope so!!!

Well darling, it's very late and I'm extra tired tonight. I went on a patrol today. Big thrill you know!

Honey, I note what you say about having sub-zero weather in Utah, and it is unusual so early in the season. Darling, I guess I'm lucky in one respect – despite the rumors – because the weather has been fairly mild so far. It isn't very cold and hardly any snow in the sector we are in. Here's hoping it will continue to be so for the remainder of the winter.

Well dearest, I'll have to close for now. Take care of yourself darling, and I hope you can have as merry a Christmas as possible. Wish your folks and family a Merry Xmas for me. Also honey, if you see any of our friends wish them the same. I'll be thinking of you darling during the holidays – even more than ever. I love and miss you so much!

Merry Christmas, honey.

With all my love,

Med

Front line troops, Korea

Entire 7th Division Ordered Back to Front Lines

28 December 1951
North Korea

Hello Darling:

    Well honey, I'm ashamed waiting so long again before writing. It's surprising how the days slip by, one after another, and me with very good intentions of writing a letter every day. As I've said before honey, every time I start a letter something unexpected turns up, especially now that the end of the year is growing near.

    It's for certain that we will have a big inspection of all our work and records for the past year and believe me, darling, we have been kept busy getting everything in shape. I didn't realize until now that our records files were in such disorder. Apparently, the old clerk wasn't as good a man as I thought he was. In any event, I'm getting very tired of the job and wish I had something else. There's a lot more to it than I thought when I first took the job. I'm not doing just my regular duties, but also anything else that these so-called wonderful officers of ours happen to think of. I can't begin to tell you all of what goes on, but it's very discouraging to do things for these high-nosed officers who seem to think they are Gods or something. Not only that, honey, but I could have taken another job recently which I know I am qualified for and made a sergeant's rating besides. I know very well that I'll never make the rating doing the job I am doing now because this particular job only calls for a corporal's rating. Well anyway, the Battery

Commander said I couldn't have the new job because he wanted me to continue on with my present one (and other reasons) so I'll probably never get another chance to make sergeant. It tees me off in a way because sergeant is a very good rank to hold now, and I know very well I could have done the job. Well darling, I'll shut up for now. I guess you get tired of hearing me complain in all my letters.

Darling, I received the beautiful Christmas card you sent and honey, let me tell you that was some card! At first, while opening it, I couldn't tell what it was because of being so large. The verse was very beautiful and well written; it expressed my sentiments exactly – towards you, darling, and I wish I could have told you so in person. As I was reading it, Lila, I was wishing how very much that I could be home with you. But then I'm always wishing that, only more so at Christmastime. Thanks very much for the card darling, and I can truthfully say that you have excellent taste in picking out cards for such occasions. I only wish that my card could have expressed to you what I wanted to say.

Honey, thank your folks also for sending me the nice card. It was very thoughtful of them, and I appreciate their remembering me. Tell them hello for me and that I wish them the best for the new year.

Well, Lila, Christmas is over and I'm glad! I'd much rather it didn't even come – being over here away from my loved ones. That's the time of the year everyone should be home with their families. I guess I needn't tell you how I felt. No kidding darling, I have never felt so low in my life. During Christmas Eve and Christmas Day all I could do was sit and think. I almost caught hell from our superiors because I didn't do my work. However, I wasn't alone, as everyone else felt the same. We had a very good dinner, as we did for Thanksgiving, but still nothing was complete. It never will be, darling, until I can be home – with you again. I hope that we won't have to spend next Christmas as we did this one.

Honey, I hope you spent as merry a Christmas as possible, and that you also enjoyed it for me. Oh, if only I could have seen a Christmas tree with lights on and all decorated up!

Darling, from the way you talked in your last letter the weather is really bad – and cold in Utah. Maybe I'm fortunate being where I am! (Big joke!) Really though, it hasn't been too awfully cold here yet, and not much snow. It's really surprising! Hope it will continue to be so.

The mail situation has been considerably slow the past two weeks – probably due to the Christmas rush. I hope it will pick up soon. I did receive a nice card from Doug & Gerrie, Mr. & Mrs. Peyton and Walt Larson today. They were late but it was good to hear from all of them.

Honey, I hope you enjoyed the Christmas party you mentioned that you were going to attend at the bank.

It's late so will have to close for this time. Happy New Year Darling, and I'll be thinking of you – as always.

With all my love, and best wishes –
Med

P.S. I'm getting along O.K. darling. Please don't worry

January 5, 1952

North Korea

Hello Darling,

How's the girl today? I hope everything is alright with you honey, and you're not working too hard.

I received two more of your sweet letters in the past few days. Honestly darling, I just can't keep up with you. Forgive me? At times I think I'm writing many letters and then I see yours coming almost every day. But Lila, I sure like it that way. You've been so sweet about writing to me ever since I came over here. No kidding, darling, I just don't know what I would do if I couldn't hear from you. Your letters have become a part of me, and without them I couldn't function properly. You know honey, some people won't write letters unless they get a prompt reply after the first one. But it isn't easy to do over here, and darling, I'm glad you understand! I try to let you know as often as I can that I'm O.K. and not to worry. I am getting along alright, so darling, please don't worry.

Well darling, how did you spend New Year's? I guess I needn't tell you how I felt. Believe me, honey, I have never felt so low in my life! The night was very exciting; the First Sergeant and I sat and looked at each other. Nice huh? I was wishing and thinking how wonderful it would have been if we could have seen the new year come in – together. But I'm not giving up hope. Maybe next year, darling. Let's hope!

Honey, I'm glad to hear that you like the earrings. It was a surprise huh? Darling, I'd give anything if I could see you now, wearing the pin and earrings. Mom said how cute you looked, but she didn't have to tell me. I know! But anyways darling, I hope you liked them, and I'll be looking forward to that special hug and kiss! I also have some for you!

Lila, I'm sorry to hear that your vase fell to pieces that you were making at the ceramics class. Don't give up honey, practice makes perfect. You're probably very good at it and won't tell me.

Congratulate your sister and husband for me. I'll bet the baby is cute. Boys always are!

Lila, I noticed that you asked me about going up front with the Infantry in one of your last letters. I guess I talk too much! Please don't worry darling, it doesn't happen very often and I'm in a safe place. I shouldn't tell you those things. I guess I don't realize what I am saying. Forgive me again?

I don't know whether I have told you this before, but after a guy has spent so much time over here, he is eligible for an R & R (Rest & Recuperation) leave to Japan for five days. My turn has finally come, so I will be leaving tomorrow. We'll travel by plane, so should get there in a short time. I wish I were coming to see you, darling, but that's just wishful thinking again. I feel as though I am cracking up. Maybe now I can see a little more of Japan, which I didn't see when I came over here.

Have you heard from Doug and Gerrie lately? I received a nice Christmas card from them but didn't get a letter.

Well darling, it's getting late again so I had better close for the time. I wanted to get this letter off tonight – before I left. I'll be thinking of and wishing that you were with me. At least I will have a rest.

Say honey, that was a really nice Christmas bonus the bank gave you. I guess the big wheels at the Walker Bank aren't so bad after all. Ha!

Well dearest, I'll close for now. Be a good girl and say hello to everyone for me.

Loving You as Always,

Med

Korean: "I Love you"
나는 당신을 사랑 하오

January 20, 1952

North Korea

Hello Darling,

    How are you honey? I hope everything is O.K. I guess you were wondering what had happened to me, and I'll admit it has been quite some time since I last wrote to you. Again, I ask your forgiveness.

    Darling, I think I told you in my last letter that I was going to Japan for a five-day R & R (Rest & Recuperation) leave. Well, I did – and have returned once more to this beloved land of Korea. Honey, I really enjoyed the leave. It seemed so good to get away from this hole for five days. But darling, I would have enjoyed it much more if you had been with me. I guess I was lucky in being able to go to Tokyo. I didn't realize it was such a big city until I started looking around and honey, a person could get lost very easily. But I did have a nice time, and the Japanese people treated us wonderfully. Honey, you will never know how good it felt to sleep in a bed again and to be able to take a bath. (A hot bath that is!) I didn't appreciate the fact of having to come back here. Honestly honey I've really felt low since I came back. All I have on my mind now is getting out of here – for good! Darling I'm thinking of you and rotation more than ever now. It just can't be too much longer!

    I've been sick lately. Nothing serious; just a bad cold. So, you see darling all this together hasn't left me with much time to write. I haven't felt like even moving for the past week, but there isn't anything to worry about. I'm feeling better now. Also darling, the plane which brought us back to Korea was late and delayed In South Korea for two days, so I didn't have a chance to write then either. Well, I've jabbered enough about that. I hope you understand what I'm trying to say.

I've received two more of your letters, honey, since returning here, and I was very anxious to hear from you. Those few days in Tokyo seemed like ages without getting a letter from you.

I'm glad Doug and Gerrie got home. They're very fortunate in being able to stay with each other like they have been. Is Gerrie going back with him this time? I hope so! Also, say hello and give them my regards. I wrote to them sometime in December but haven't heard from them since. Hope they received my letter.

Darling, conditions here are about the same. The war is still going on, and everything looks the same. I will soon be starting on my 9th month in Korea. I think that's about enough, don't you? No kidding I'm getting so tired of this place that I'm almost out of my mind. Everyday it's the same thing over and over, and if people only knew of some of the things we must put up with, meaning of course, the Officers and big wheels! SHUT UP MED! There I go again.

Well darling how is everything with you? You're not working too hard, are you? You hadn't better be!

Darling, I want you to be in top condition when I get home. Ha! (I know you will be). Well Lila, it's late again, and I'm tired as usual. Maybe I'm run down huh? I'll write more next time. Tell everyone hello, and don't worry honey, I'm O.K.

Loving you as always, darling,

Med

R & R in Tokyo, Japan

January 26, 1952

North Korea

Hello Darling,

 Well honey, how is everything? I hope all is well with you and your family. Darling, I think about you so often that I don't have time for anything else, and that's the way I like it! The more time I spend with you (in my thoughts) the less time I must think about what's going on over here. And darling, believe me, it isn't good to think about this hellhole very much. It's bad enough just being here!

 Honey, I received two more of your ever-welcomed letters lately. I'm always so happy to hear from you. You know darling, you are about the only one that writes to me anymore. Suddenly everyone stopped! Maybe they figure that I don't write to them enough. I don't know. But I do know that I've answered everyone's letter that has written to me so far. The mail can easily become lost, and I think that's what happened. I think if a person spent some time over here, they would realize just how conditions are, and that it isn't easy to be writing letters all the time when expected. I'm not saying this to you, darling, because I think you do understand what I'm saying, and you've been very sweet about writing to me ever since I got here. I couldn't ask for more and darling, I do love and admire you for writing the way you have. Lila, I've always had your letters to look forward to whether anyone else wrote or not, and believe me honey, yours are the most important to me! If I can hear from you, I don't care about anything else.

Well darling, I think I told you in the last letter of my visit to Tokyo, Japan, and it did seem so nice to be where there was peace and quiet again. Anyway, it seemed so nice that I didn't want to go back to Korea. Darling, I don't know what got into me, but I went A.W.O.L. (over the hill) in Japan. Honey, I know that I'm no different from any other guy over here, but I just couldn't see coming back to Korea. I've never felt that way before. Anyway honey, my freedom didn't last too long because I did come back, and of course I must be punished. I was given trial by Court-martial yesterday. Maybe I'm making it sound too severe, but it really wasn't. I could have been reduced to a Private again, but I wasn't. But I did get a fine – 30 days restriction to the area, and five days hard labor. My offense really wasn't too serious, as the same thing happens all the time. Even Officers take more time than they should on their R & R leaves to Japan. Darling, please don't think too badly of me, will you? I guess anyone can get out of line occasionally. I wanted to tell you in the last letter, but I thought maybe my punishment would be more serious. If it had been, I wouldn't have told you because you would only worry. Everything is alright now honey, so please don't worry about me. I'll bet you think I'm a little devil, don't you? Well, maybe I am!

My chances for making Sergeant are gone now, so honey, I guess I'll be a little old Corporal for the rest of my time in the Army. How about that? Darling, when I get home, you'll have to clue me in for pulling a stunt like that, huh? And honey, please don't say anything to the folks. They're very much one-way and would only make a mountain out of a molehill.

Darling, it's getting late again, and I've talked so much about my crazy actions that I don't have enough time to talk to you about anything else. You know me, it takes three pages to bring out one little thought.

I guess Doug has left by this time but say hello to Gerrie for me. Maybe sometime Doug and I will be lucky enough to be home at the same time. I hope the snow isn't too deep. I'd sure hate to see you get snowed in.

Darling, I'm just passing an opinion, but I expect to rotate sometime in March. It wasn't definite honey so don't quote me on it. However, it can't be too awfully long because there are only 13 men ahead of me. Oh darling, I hope they don't let me down!

Well, be good and say hello to everyone. Don't worry honey, I'm getting along alright. You sure look cute tonight! Don't tell me I can't see you because I can! (Old memories, you know).

With all my love, Darling,

Med

February 2, 1952

North Korea

Hello Lover,

Well honey, I have a few minutes before bedtime, so I thought I would write a few lines to let you know that I'm still O.K. and getting along alright.

Darling, I received a letter from you yesterday and noticed that it had been quite some time since you had heard from me. Honey, please forgive me because I was all riled-up and upset after my court-martial. I wanted to write sooner, but I just didn't feel up to it. Please understand darling, and I promise to do better in the future. My little episode is all forgotten now, so everything is alright.

Guess what honey? You know I mentioned that I was given five days hard labor? Well, I had to dig a hole, 6' x 6', plus a few other foolish things. How about that? Honey, it does seem stupid, but I guess digging a hole occasionally won't hurt anyone.

Well darling, there really isn't too much to say about conditions over here. They haven't changed any since the last letter, except that two more men have rotated from our outfit. Each one puts me that much closer. I'm still counting very strongly on getting out of here sometime in March.

Tomorrow I will be starting my 9th month in Korea, and darling, I think that's about enough, don't you?

Honestly, when I think back through the long old months, I just don't see how I survived this long. But honey, I think it was due to your many wonderful letters, which have come so regularly. I don't think I would have made it without them. There isn't any need to worry now, darling, because it can't be too much longer before I can be with you again. The time is going fast now and before you know it, we will be together again.

Darling, that 30 days leave which I will get when I get home will really be appreciated by me. Just think, honey, 30 long days. It sounds wonderful to me. How about you?

From the way it sounds you really must be having a severe winter in Utah. It would have to be to drive the deer down from the mountains like you mentioned in your letter. Darling, I should have been there with my rifle because that's the only way I can get one, unless a deer is staring me in the face, I can never hit one.

Darling, how is your car running? Does it still leak anti-freeze? Honey don't feel badly about that because I did the same thing one time. We only learn by experience you know! Honey, if the truth was known I'll bet you are a real good mechanic by now. But take it easy, darling, and don't get in any races.

How is Gerrie feeling since Doug left? I can well imagine because I felt the same when I left you, darling. Tell her hello for me.

Oh, honey, I'm very proud of you getting the promotion in the bank. You're really alright, darling, and no one deserved it more than "my girl".

I'll have to close for now. Be good honey. I'll write again soon.

With all my Love, Me

February 9, 1952

North Korea

Hello My Dearest,

Well honey, how are things going? I hope everything is alright with you and your family.

Darling, I received the very beautiful valentine and want to express my thanks and appreciation once more for your everlasting thoughtfulness. Honey, you sure have a talent for picking out beautiful cards, and the verses are just out of this world! Honestly darling, I'd give anything if I could express myself the way the authors of those cards do. But Lila, I want you to know that I feel the same towards you – as each word that valentine said. Honey, I only wish that I were with you now so I could tell you in person. Thanks again darling, and I love you very much for it.

I also received another of your ever-inspiring letters today. All your letters are nice, honey, but there just seemed to be something special about this one. It seemed, almost, as if we were side by side talking to each other, and darling, it does get me excited and bothered. Lila, you say some of the sweetest things, which make me very happy. I'm glad you feel the way you do darling, because I assure you that I feel the same – and those feelings are growing stronger every day.

I'm just living now for the day that the big "R" (Rotation) rolls around. When the time does come, I'll be so happy that I won't know which end my head is on. It's been so long since I've been happy that I'll probably get lost in my emotions. But who cares, honey, I'll have a good reason – don't you think? We can get lost together, huh?

Darling, I'm glad that you didn't think too badly of me for pulling the little stunt I did over here. I realize now it was foolish, but no need worrying about it now. I guess anyone can get out of line occasionally. Especially men!

Honey, you asked about the five days hard labor, which I received. Well, it sounds silly, but I had to dig a few holes in the ground, such as: sumps and fox holes, of which the latter is sometimes needed. It did tee me off at first, until I realized that there would be no point in making an issue of it. I've been in the Army long enough to know that it doesn't pay to argue with superiors. I thought it best to shut up and dig!

I'm getting along alright now, darling, so please don't worry. Everything is O.K.!

Is the new job at the bank going alright? I'll bet you're

doing a terrific job. Anything you do, honey, I know is done well. I'm very proud of you. How does it feel to be a big wheel? Ha!

Well darling, I've almost run out of things to say for tonight, so had better close. Conditions are the same, and I still think I should get out of here sometime in March.

Did Gerrie get a job at the bank? Take it easy honey. I'll write again soon.

With Everlasting Love, Darling,

Med

February 21, 1952

North Korea

Hi Honey,

Well darling, how is every little thing? It had better be alright!

Darling, I've been thinking about you lately – ever so much. Honey, as I've said before, you have always been with me over here, but lately I've thought about you more than usual. If it's possible! You know, Lila, I think it's because I know that it won't be too much longer before I see you. The nearer the time comes to my being rotated, the more anxious I become. It's been a very long time, darling, and you've been very patient – waiting so long. I love you so much, Lila, I just don't know what I would have done if you hadn't have waited.

Darling, I knew how I felt towards you when I was home last time, but I guess I just didn't know how to say it. You know, honey, I wanted to say so much to you before I left, but the words just weren't there. I hope you understand what I'm trying to say now. Believe me, honey, I'll do a better job when I get home this time! There are many things I want to say – and ask you, darling. You know the old saying "Absence makes the heart grow fonder." Well, it sure did for me. You'll never know! And darling, it makes me very happy that you feel the way you do. Nothing can make me happier than to be rotated and come back to you.

As far as I know next month will be the time. Lately we have sent three more men home, and I am now number seven on the list. However, I still have two weeks to go before completing nine months. But honey, the time will go fast and any time after nine months I will be eligible. I think maybe the middle of March should find me on my way. Let's hope, darling.

Honey, I don't know if you know Bob Niederhauser or not, but we finally got to see each other. He must have gotten my address from his wife, who knows Gerrie. It came as a big surprise because I didn't think I would ever see him after so long a time. Bob arrived in Korea almost a month ahead of me and is now on his way home. It seemed nice to see an old friend, and I enjoyed the visit with him before he left. You know, honey, he had been in the same division, in a signal company located to the rear, and I didn't get a chance to talk to him before this. It's funny how you can be so near a person over here and not even know he is around. But then I guess that's always the case where a war is going on; everyone is constantly on the move and unsettled.

Me and my rifle

Front Line Tents

We've been doing a little moving ourselves lately. Our Battalion has moved back to the central front again. We traveled 100 miles in open trucks and believe me, it was cold! I spent the first night thawing out. I felt almost like an ice cube. Everything is alright now, and I sure hope this will be my last move. It's very uncomfortable and miserable traveling through these mountains on narrow dirt roads with scarcely enough room for two vehicles to pass.

Well honey, I'm finding it difficult thinking of something to say tonight, so perhaps I'd better give up for now.

There has been a mail shortage lately, which has limited my mail to one letter in over a week. But darling, I know they will get through soon, and I'll be ever so anxious to hear from you. I know it isn't your fault, honey. It's just the damn mail system.

How is Gerrie getting along? Did she get a job at the bank? Also honey I've been wondering where and what Doug is doing. I haven't heard from him for so long that I was beginning to wonder.

Well darling, I'll close for now. Say hello to everyone.

With all my Love, Med

A typical officer's jeep

March 1, 1952

North Korea

Hello My Darling,

Well honey, I hope everything is going alright with you. I've been thinking of you so much lately and hoping that conditions are about the same as usual.

Darling, in the past week I have received several more of your ever inspiring letters. You know honey, for a while there I thought I had almost caught up with my letter writing, but now I'm way behind again. I guess it's just impossible! Nevertheless darling, I want you to know how very much your letters are appreciated; they mean everything in the world to me. Without them these nine months in Korea would have been much lonelier. You know honey, three of your letters came the same day, and because we have been moving so much lately, somehow, they got lost, so I didn't remember everything you asked about or wanted to know. I do read every one of your letters very carefully. I finally gave up trying to keep all your letters, honey, because there just wasn't room enough to carry them. I think I could have filled a suitcase with just letters.

Darling, I'm still hoping that we won't have to write too much longer. Although it is the only means of communication over here, but still, it isn't like seeing you – and talking to you in person. At times I'm filled with inspiration to such a point that I could write a book, and then when the time comes to put it on paper, my mind is blank. So that explains, honey, why I sometimes spend two or more hours on one letter. Maybe I've been over here too long, huh?

Well darling, tomorrow I will have nine months in Korea, and rotation is operating on a full-time schedule, so it's my guess that I will leave here sometime within the next two to three weeks. I am number four on the list, so I can't possibly see how I will be here too much longer.

Honey, in one of your letters you asked if the releasing of the National Guard personnel would have any bearing on my rotation? As far as I know and have heard, it won't affect me, for I should be out of here before many National Guardsmen are released. I hope!

Darling, because of my replacement getting here too early and me with nothing to do, I have been put back in a gun section until I go home. I don't care much for the big guns, especially now after being away from them for so long, but I guess I can stand it for a while. You know honey, after getting a replacement, you are treated just like dirt – just as though you weren't even around. It doesn't do much good to argue; I'll just have to do it!

Well dearest, it's almost time for me to go on duty and I am exceptionally lost for words tonight.

How is the new job going honey? I hope they aren't working you too hard. Please don't let them!

Is the bad weather almost over now? From what I

have heard Utah is having a severe winter again. I hope it is almost over. I think the worst part of the winter is over here, and I'm glad. It's miserable moving around in the snow.

Well darling I'll close for now. Say hello to everyone for me. I'm hoping and praying honey that it won't be much longer before we see each other again.

Be good darling and take it easy.

With all my love, as always,

Med

P.S. Forgive me, Lila honey, but I forgot to mention the nice package you sent. I'm very absent minded, huh? Thanks darling, it was sweet of you. I always enjoy eating candy and the cigarettes will come in handy going home.

---

13 March 1952

Sasebo, Japan

Hello Darling,

Well honey, I'm sorry that I have neglected my letter writing lately, but I've been terribly busy. Honey, guess what? I'm on my way home! It came as a complete surprise to me as they only gave me a few hours' notice to get ready. I left my outfit in Korea the morning of the

6 th and arrived in Sasebo, Japan yesterday. We've been kept busy processing at every Camp on the way. I didn't realize there was so much red tape involved in being rotated to the States, but honey, it's well worth it!! I can't tell you what a wonderful feeling it is to know that I'm coming home again!

Many of the boys won't return but I'm sure they won't have died in vain. I just hope that it won't be too much longer before they can all return.

Darling, I'm getting more anxious each day to see you, and if I'm lucky I will see you in three or four weeks from now. I'm not sure when we will leave here, but it should be within the next few days. I don't know whether we will dock at San Francisco or Washington as the ships have been going both places. I'll call you as soon as I reach the States.

This letter will have to be short. I won't get a chance to write again but don't worry, it won't be long now! I'll see you soon.

With all my love darling, Med

P.S. Please don't write back.

Entire 7th Division Ordered Back to Front Lines

Home on leave – married!

Mr. and Mrs. Floyd A. Hansen

announce the marriage

of their daughter

Lila Mae

to

Medford Dee Poulsen

son of Mr. and Mrs. H. O. Poulsen

on Saturday, the twenty-sixth day of April

nineteen hundred and fifty-two

Las Vegas, Nevada

at Home
1904 East 17th South
Salt Lake City, Utah

May 11, 1952
Sunday

My Dearest Wife:

Well, darling, I hope this letter will find you in better spirits than myself.

Honey, talking to you on the phone last night meant everything in the world to me — but when I had to say good-bye and hang up — well, that was almost

CHAPTER 8

The Final Chapter
Camp Carson, Colorado

"Oh honey, I love you! I love you!
I love you! If only I could see and
be near you — even for a few minutes."

May 11, 1952 — Sunday

My Dearest Wife,

    Well darling, I hope this letter finds you in better spirits than myself. Honey, talking to you on the phone last night meant everything in the world to me – but when I had to say good-bye and hang up – well, that was almost more than I could stand! Oh Lila, I love and miss you so much that I'm almost out of my mind. It just doesn't seem fair that we should have to be separated. I just keep turning over and over in my mind the idea of staying in this hole for four months. Darling let's hope and pray that the Army won't change their decision again and let me out on schedule.

    Oh honey, I love you! I love you! I love you! If only I could see and be near you – even for a few minutes. Darling, I have one regret, and that is that I wish we would have been married sooner during my 30-day leave. But we will have a wonderful lifetime together if only we can get through these four months. You're a wonderful little wife and I love, admire and respect you more than I thought I could any girl. Honey don't laugh when I say this – I'd die for you! You're all in the world that I want and I'm so happy that you did become my wife. Darling don't ever change! Please don't ever change your feelings towards me. I couldn't stand it! As I told you before I left, you are the only girl for me and always will be.

The Final Chapter Camp Carson, Colorado

Lila darling, please don't ever lose your faith and trust in me, although I know you do have a reason because of my actions in Japan. Darling, believe me when I say that I don't have any desire to ever go astray again. Each day that goes by makes me realize what a sweet and wonderful girl you are, and I'm proud to be your husband!

Honey, I guess you remember that guy from Morgan, Utah whom I went overseas with? Well, I met him here yesterday, so I feel a little better than I did at first. He and I went to Colorado Springs last night just to get away from this Camp. That's where I called you from. I'm not quite certain whether he or even myself will be stationed here, but there is every indication that we will. I hope we will be near each other anyway.

Darling, I looked at several hotels in Colorado Springs. The rooms are nice and clean but also expensive. Honey, I think we could plan for you to come and even stay a week sometime, which would mean everything to me. What do you think honey? Do you think the bank would let you have another week off sometime this summer? It couldn't be for a while because I may not even stay here. Think it over darling and let me know.

The Camp here is quite nice but also lonely. There isn't much activity because most of the men stationed here live close by and can go home every weekend. That's why it is so lonely. But I guess the only thing to do is shut up and take it.

I'm glad you sold the car honey for the price you

wanted. I hope it won't inconvenience you too much. Darling, we'll get one as soon as I am out. Did the record come from Nevada yet? If not honey, why don't you write them a letter? I'm glad that you remembered my mother on Mother's Day, and I hope they'll understand that I didn't have any time. Darling, please see my mother as often as you can because she does think the world of you, and it may help her to get well.

Well darling, there isn't much more to say for now. Please take care of yourself and above all don't work too hard! And honey, don't lose any weight. I'd like you to be just the way you were when I came home.

Please write real soon and tell me everything. I'll be here for quite some time, so I'll get the letters. Say hello to your folks and family for me. Honey, if anyone wants to know why I haven't written tell them that I'll write when I'm permanently assigned. I'm going to write the folks now also.

Darling, I'm going to try and call you at least once a week for a while. It doesn't cost too much, and I should get paid tomorrow. Oh Lila, I hate to close this letter, but I'll have to, but will write again soon. You do the same honey. Your letters mean everything to me. Be good darling, and I love you with all my heart. You cute little shit!

With Deepest of Love, Your husband,

Med

May 12, 1952

My Darling Wife,

Well honey, I haven't written for two days so thought I'd write a few lines tonight. Honey, I received your letter and the income tax statement yesterday. I'm going to sign it and send it back tonight. Thanks a lot honey, it was sweet of you to take care of it for me. I can always depend on my little wife! I'd sure like to give you a big smooch, but I guess that will have to wait as much as I hate to. Honey, you'd better watch out when I get home again! I'll probably eat you up! I keep thinking how nice it will be to be able to hold you again. Sometimes, honey, I could almost go crazy. Oh, if the next few months don't hurry and pass, I don't know what I'll do. The time is going so terribly slow. Each day seems like a week!

Darling, you remember I said there may be a possibility of getting out early. Well don't count on it because it was all just a heartbreaking rumor. You hear so many damn false stories around here that it just isn't safe to let yourself believe anything. There isn't anything much we can do about it, but it's sure discouraging having to live like this. Darling, I'll be so happy the day I get discharged that I won't know how to act. The world will be ours, honey. We can be together always; do what we want – and no one will be telling us how to live. I'm just living for that day and that day only! I hope it will soon come!

Darling, I told you that my trouble had taken a turn for the worse. I went to the doctor again yesterday. He said not to get discouraged and worry too much about it because my condition isn't nearly as serious as it was at first. He seems to think that it will heal up entirely when I once settle down to a normal married life. I think you know what I mean, honey. We won't need to rush ourselves as much as we did when I was home. And we both need practice. What do you think? How is the weather there honey? I imagine it's hot, but it couldn't be quite as bad as this hellhole. It was nearly 100 degrees today. Pretty warm huh? You know how easy it is for me to perspire. You should have seen me today! I looked like I'd been dunked in a swimming pool.

Well honey, I hope you're not working too hard, and everything is alright with you and your family. You'd better be a good girl and take care of yourself for me. I want you in top shape when I get home.

I'm sending a $60 money order. It isn't too awful much but will help. I guess money is money huh?

I'll close for now, darling, but will write again soon.

With All My Love, Your Husband Med

P.S. Lila, there's been a slight change in address, so copy it as I have it on this letter.

13 May 1952

My Darling Wife,

Well honey, it's me again. There really isn't much to say but I thought I would write a few lines to let you know that everything is O.K., except of course, that I still feel the same towards the Army and I'm still very lonely – and love and miss you more than ever.

Oh Lila, I'm so homesick to see you that I could go crazy. You're on my mind constantly from one day's end to the other. I keep thinking of the wonderful 30 days we spent together and how happy I am that we were married. I'll never forget the week we spent at the "Spiking Motor Lodge", if I live to be 100 years old. Oh darling, it was wonderful! You made me so happy, and I'll always love and cherish each memory of that week.

Lila darling, you're wonderful! I couldn't have found any girl to equal you if I'd have searched the world over. I hope we can always be happy and believe me, honey, I'll do my very best.

Honey, I guess you remember in our last telephone conversation my so-called "condition" had gotten worse. It is honey – much worse! The last two days I have spent trying to get an appointment with a Urologist here on the Post but haven't succeeded yet. Honey, they just don't seem to care what happens to a person. My condition is more serious than before and quite painful, but what do they care? I guess I overworked and strained myself again honey, which I knew would happen. But I'm not sorry! I love you so much that it just didn't matter. Please don't worry too much about it because I will get to see the doctor one of these days. I just hope it won't develop into anything serious before that time!

Well darling, everything is about the same. I haven't been reassigned yet and don't know when I will be. The Army doesn't need us men here anymore than the man in the moon does. Most all the guys are just laying around doing nothing. I can't understand why they don't turn us loose now. However, some of them are getting out early, so honey, let's keep our fingers crossed that a break may come my way for a change. Oh honey, I'd be so happy if I could get out right away. I guess we both would!

I wrote you a letter the day before yesterday. Hope you received it.

Darling, have you seen the picture of us in the paper yet? Be sure to tell me all about it. I'm very anxious to hear all about the bridal showers and such as that.

Well darling, I'll close for now. Don't work too hard and take it easy! Say hello to everyone for me.

Your Ever-loving Husband,

Med

The Final Chapter Camp Carson, Colorado

MARRIED IN NEVADA RITES
Cpl. and Mrs. Medford Dee Poulsen, wed recently in Las Vegas, Nev. ceremony. The bride is the former Miss Lila Mae Hansen.

Lila Mae Hansen Is Married In Colorful Nevada Rites

Miss Lila Mae Hansen and Cpl. Medford Dee Poulsen exchanged wedding vows recently at the "Hitching Post" Chapel in Las Vegas.

The bride is a daughter of Mr. and Mrs. Floyd A. Hansen, 1904 E. 17th South.

Cpl. Poulsen, a field artilleryman who saw combat in Korea, is a son of Mr. and Mrs. H. C. Poulsen, 536 Leland Ave.

Mr. and Mrs. Jay W. Galli were the best man and matron of honor at the wedding ceremony.

The bride wore a street length gown of navy blue and white organdy and a white shell hat. Her corsage was of white carnations.

After a honeymoon in Las Vegas and Zion National Park, the bride returned to Salt Lake City, and the bridegroom reported back to Camp Carson, Colo., for reassignment.

Following his release from military service, the couple will make a home in Salt Lake City.

The couple was honored at a dinner at the Hansen home Tuesday evening.

May 16, 1952

Hello My Darling Wife,

    Well honey, I received the two wonderful letters yesterday and today, and I can't begin to tell you how thrilled and happy I was to receive them. I was getting so anxious and worried that I could hardly wait. Honestly honey, I've read them a dozen times and each time they mean more to me. I can just picture you talking, and that cute little grin and wink which you are so free with. Oh, Lila, I'd give anything if I could see you – even for a few minutes! But darling, I guess conditions just won't permit, especially with me in the condition I am. I told you in one of my previous letters that it had gotten much worse since I came back here. Oh darling, believe me when I say that I want to see you more than anything in the world, but it just wouldn't be sensible at the present time. If we were together now, darling, you know what would happen and so do I. (We'd have a session!)

Darling, I finally got started taking treatments from the Army Urologist here on the Post, and he said that in my present condition any excitement such as I stated above would be the worst thing I could do! I'm not saying this just to be talking but it is serious, and I want you to know. I'm taking drugs, therapy treatments and such as that. He seems to be a good doctor honey, so please don't worry too much. It's going to take time, and I won't be able to drink coffee or liquor for six months to a year, so he says. Darling, there are several other guys taking treatments for the same thing, so please don't think I'm the only one. He said that chances are the condition will remain with me (off and on) for the rest of my life. Oh darling, I'm sorry! I've never had anything hurt me so much in my life. Not physically – I mean mentally!! It isn't fair to you. Lila, I love you so much that I just couldn't live without you. Oh darling, please forgive me! I'll do anything to correct my mistake.

Please give me a chance, honey! Maybe I'll get over it; let's hope and pray. I just hope that I won't ever have to undergo an operation. That would be serious!

Honey, I was sure thrilled with the pictures, and the articles were very nice. Honey, you sure looked sweet in the picture of you alone. I'm proud of you darling. You're the most wonderful little wife a guy could ever have.

The announcement was very nice also. I'll bet that was a big job, huh? Honey, I wish we could have sent one to everyone in Salt Lake, because I want everyone to know who I married. I'm so proud of you honey!

Honey, I can't help but think how miserable Gerrie is making herself. I guess Marilyn doesn't know what to think of her either, huh? Don't worry about it darling; she'll get over it someday. I still think it's jealousy, and I believe it more now than before because Bob and I were home on leave, and I guess she felt bad because Doug wasn't. I don't blame her, but she doesn't have to act so stinky.

I hope you and Marilyn enjoyed the show, and I think you should go often honey. Say hello to Marilyn for me.

Yes honey, I'm glad you sold the car. That would have been a shame if those damn kids would have hit it. I hope they didn't damage your property too much.

Honey, I'm signing this card from the Walker Bank, and don't you dare laugh if it's in the wrong place, you cute little shit you! Seriously darling, I think a joint account is a good idea. When I die you can withdraw all the money without going through too much red tape. Ha!

Darling, I haven't heard from mom and dad yet, and I can't figure out why because I wrote to them when I wrote to you the first time. I hope they're not mad at me. I'm anxious to hear because I've been worrying about mom. Give them the word, honey, will you?

Well darling, there isn't anything new to say for this time. I love you so terribly much and I'm just living for the day, we can be together again. Write soon and tell me about the bridal shower. Take good care of yourself, darling, and say hello to everyone for me. I'll write again soon.

With my deepest of Love,

Your Husband,

Med

May 21, 1952

Hello Darling,

Lila, I'm sorry that I didn't get a letter written last night but after I called you honey, I went back to the barracks and washed out some clothes. I've been putting it off for a week and they began to pile up, so I spent last evening washing them. Forgive me?

Oh darling, you just don't know how much that phone call thrilled me. Just to hear your voice and be able to talk to you thrills me so very much. Honestly honey, I felt wonderful – but it soon wears off. It doesn't take long to realize that it was just a phone call and I'm not with you! Lila, honey, I just don't know how I'm going to stay away from you until August. It seems so long and far distant that I hate to even think about it. Darling, I'm counting the days as they go by and believe me, they are slow!

Lila, I'm so very much in love with you, and I doubt if you can realize just how much I do love you. My love for you grows – and darling, it is a wonderful feeling to know that I have such a sweet and loving little wife waiting for my return.

Honey let's hope and pray that my enlistment won't be extended again. As I've said so many times before, I couldn't stand it! Darling, I'm so lonely again that I hardly know what to do with myself. I told you that my buddy was shipped out yesterday and I'm all alone again. It made me feel much better being with him, and he has been a very good friend to me. I hope that some more of my friends will come through here because it does help a great deal.

Darling, I guess I'm very sentimental, but hearing some of the popular songs on the juke box in the P.X. that were played while I was home brings back so many wonderful memories. Songs such as: "Blue Tango,"

"Blacksmith Blues," "When I Look into your Eyes," and several others. I'm completely engrossed in my thoughts when I hear them. But darling, I've also heard another on which I didn't hear when I was home. It's called "Half As Much" by Rosemary Clooney. I think it's very pretty. The words especially. Have you heard it honey? If not, please do. I'm sure you will agree with me. Darling, I always think of you when I hear it.

I'm glad the record finally came. Darling, please don't wear it out; I'm counting very much on hearing it, but I realize how much it means to us and I would probably do the same thing. Do you think it would be possible to have another one made? Then you could play it all you want. Do all our folks like the record? How about the picture, honey? Have you had any more made? When you do, please give one to my dad to send to Ona, or else I can.

It really doesn't matter. Darling, have you had the rings fixed yet? Maybe I'm asking too many questions. You'll probably have to write a book answering them all. It's getting late, so I better close for now. Don't worry about me, honey, I think I'm getting much better. You take real good care of yourself, won't you? Say hello to your dad.

Your Ever-Loving Husband,
Med

May 26, 1952

Hello Doll,

How's everything, honey? I hope you're getting along alright and not working too hard.

Darling, I received another of your ever welcome letters today, and the very beautiful anniversary card. Thanks, honey – thanks for being so thoughtful! Darling, the verse is very touching. I've read it over and over all day. Although our anniversary can't be too happy under the circumstances, darling, I want you to know that the card does mean so much to me. It makes me happy to know that we have been married for one month today. Lila, I still wish that we would have been married sooner, but darling, I shouldn't be telling you. I'm the one who should have proposed. Darling, it isn't that I didn't want to, I guess maybe I just didn't know how to go about it. But honey, I do feel wonderful and I'm more thankful each day – that you are my wife. Somehow darling, I feel more at ease and content, even though we aren't together. Just knowing that you're my wife – and that you'll be waiting when I get home, that's all I care about, darling. I won't guarantee how long I'll be able to stay away from you, but I will try and make the most of it. Believe me Lila, it isn't easy – and I'm sure you feel the same.

Oh honey, I'm so lonely that I hardly know what to do with myself! Honestly darling, I didn't ever think that

I could love any girl as much as I love you! You're on my mind constantly, from one day's end to the other. Don't ever let anything happen to you darling. If I couldn't come home to you – I wouldn't want to come home at all! I hope I can always keep you happy. I'll try, darling! I'll do anything!

Are the showers over yet? I can imagine how they must have kept you going. Gee honey, I'll bet you did get a lot of nice things. I can hardly wait until I see them all.

Darling, you mentioned how tired and worn out you were, and I can well imagine how you must have been. When you feel that way honey, I'll understand if you don't write every night. Don't stay up all night trying to write a letter if you don't feel up to it. As much as I appreciate them honey, I don't want you to over-do yourself. Darling, in case you were wondering about my condition, it is improving a great deal. I feel much better, for it was making me sick at times. I went to the doctor again today and he seems to think that a rest will do me good. If I take it easy, he says that I should be well cured by the time I get discharged. But he also said not to overlook the fact that it can come back at any time. But at the present time I am much better, so honey please don't worry. I'll let you know from time to time how I am getting along. He also said a little beer wouldn't hurt me now, so I had a beer tonight. How about that?

Darling, you asked about my job and how I was getting along. Well honey, it's just ordinary administrative work such as I was doing overseas. Keeping records, typing out various rosters and correspondence, making out passes and furlough papers for the men. That's about it. It is a good job, but I'm sure that I would appreciate it more under conditions other than the Army. You know what I mean? It also has its advantages. I don't have to stand in the chow line, which is ordinarily a block long. I have a special pass because of my job, which permits me to go in the mess hall ahead of the crowd. So, that isn't too bad, huh? Usually, a job of this sort helps you to get acquainted with the wheels, and that means a great deal in the Army.

How is the weather there, darling? It rains and blows here almost every day, and believe me, it is getting tiresome. I hope summer will get here soon! Honey, have you seen Dick and Nellie lately? I wrote them a letter quite some time ago, but no answer yet. I hope they haven't forgotten me already! Well darling, there isn't much more to say for now, except that I'm still loving and missing you as much as always. I will have been here three weeks Wednesday, so the time is passing, slow but sure. Take it easy, darling, and tell everyone hello for me. I'll write again soon.

Your Ever-Loving Husband,

Med

30 May 1952

Hello Darling,

How are you doing, honey? I'm sorry that I haven't written sooner this week, but honestly honey, I've tried! I started a letter last night but just couldn't finish. I sat here for a solid hour trying to write. It didn't work out, so I gave up and went to a show.

Darling, it's getting so lately I can't even think straight anymore. I just can't seem to think or concentrate without difficulty.

As I said before, this camp is just like a ghost town. There's no one around, no place to go, and nothing to do. Day follows day in a cycle of drudgery. Honestly Lila, I'm going crazy! I wish now that I would have been shipped out of here because then I would have been assigned to a regular outfit and had a permanent job every day. The time passes faster that way. Although I do have a job here – and a good one – I still have too much free time.

Another thing honey, I am in the same barracks with the men that are being discharged. Believe me, it isn't easy to sit here and see all these guys being discharged every day.

Darling, I received two more of your ever-loving letters the past two days. If it wasn't for them, I know I would lose my mind. Please don't think I'm being foolish because there are so many other guys here who feel the same way. I've heard several of them say that they wish they were still in Korea. In a way, I do too honey, because then I could have gotten out as soon as I reached the States. If only I could have stayed in Korea two more months. Then I would have been discharged as soon as I got back.

Well honey, today is a holiday. I've sat here all day just thinking how nice it would be if we were together. Darling, I miss you so much that I just can't stand it anymore! Oh, how I wish they would let me out before August! It is still almost three months away, isn't it? I promise you that these three months will seem like an eternity.

Darling, it was sweet of you to want to get on the train and come here for the weekend. As much as I want to see you, honey, I don't think it would be wise. I'm sure you understand. I am getting much better, but it wouldn't take much at all to start it all over again. I think it best to rest for a while, don't you?

If anyone wonders why you don't come here to see me, think of something to tell them, will you? You know how people are. They'd probably wonder what the scoop was. I'm not saying this just to scare you, honey, but two weeks ago when my trouble was so bad, I passed some blood a time or two through my you know where. Believe me darling, I was scared! So, you see it must have been pretty serious. I don't want that to happen again and I'm sure you don't either. So, Lila, let's try to wait. I know it isn't easy for either of us, but we'll just have to. I think I'm almost well again, so please don't worry or get alarmed about what I tell you because it hasn't happened again.

Honey, did you ever get those pictures developed that we took on our honeymoon? I've been wondering how they turned out. I'd sure like to see them.

Well darling, I'll close for now. Be good and take care of yourself.

Your loving husband,

Med

June 2, 1952

Hello Darling,

Well honey, this the 3rd attempt I've made at trying to write a letter tonight. It isn't that I don't want to write, honey, believe me! I just can't seem to accomplish anything lately. I've never felt so lonely and downhearted in my life! Honestly darling, I don't know how I'm going to stand it until August. This feeling seems to grow worse every day. If only I knew someone here – a good friend to talk to and run around with. But I don't! Everywhere I go and everything I do – I do alone. But that's just a small part of it. I'm forever yearning and longing to be near you again. Honey, I've relived (within myself) every minute of that last wonderful week we were together. I'd give anything if we were sharing the same joy and companionship right now! Darling, it just doesn't seem fair that we should have to be separated like this. I didn't realize that this old world was so cruel. Darling, it's torture – and sometimes mental torture is much worse than physical.

Oh honey, if you only knew how great the temptation is – to just say "to hell with everything," and jump on a plane and come home to you. Believe me when I say I want to, more than anything in this world. I could over a weekend, but it would only be for a day or so, but then when I would have to leave you again and come back here, it would hurt me more than ever. Please understand my feelings darling and try to bear with me. I know it's hard for both of us but honestly, honey, I don't think there is a person on this earth lonelier than I am. I feel as though the whole world deserted me and left me here to die. Please don't think I'm talking foolish honey, because I'm not. I'm very serious. As I've said before darling, I couldn't live without you, and I realize it more each day. That's why I feel the way I do because I'm not with you. The next time I see you honey, I don't want to ever leave you again. Under no conditions – none whatsoever! I hope you feel the same, darling. You'd better you cute little shit!

In the past two days I have received two more of your wonderful letters, and I note what you say about not hearing from me in five days. I'm really sorry, honey.

Honest I am! I had no intentions of letting it go that long. Like I told you – I've tried to write more, but I just couldn't. I have to get up and move or I'll go crazy. Please accept my weak excuse honey, for that's the only one I can offer. But it's true! I'll promise to do better in the future.

Well darling, there isn't much more to say for this time. Don't worry about me, I'm getting along O.K. You take it easy yourself and don't overwork!

I'm glad you and Marilyn Niederhauser are getting out occasionally. It will do you both good. Say hello to Marilyn for me.

I'll try to call you Thursday or Friday of this week. Be good honey. I'll have to close for now.

With the deepest of Love,

Your Husband Med

P.S. Darling, don't think that I've said some foolish things in this letter. It's entirely the way I feel, and I can't help it. I miss you so much. Believe me, Lila, this letter was written from my heart.

June 5, 1952

Hi Lover,

I received another letter today darling, and I was as thrilled as ever to hear from you. You know honey, I didn't get one yesterday and I was completely lost. It's sort of a routine now, because I usually get one every day at the same time.

I'm not complaining darling, but just giving you an idea of what your letters mean to me! You've been very sweet about writing to me, and always have been. I guess I should talk huh? Especially when you didn't hear from me in five days. But honey, I tried to explain in my last letter what the scoop was. I honestly tried to write, but like I said before – if you don't get up and move around or go to a show or something, you'd go crazy. I guess no one can realize just how dull this place really is. You have to be here to find out.

Darling, I was sorry to hear that those pictures didn't turn out. I too am disappointed. But don't feel bad honey, I couldn't have loaded the camera any better. We can take some more when I get home, but it would have been nice to see those pictures of Boulder Dam and Zions, huh? I would have liked to have seen the one of us smooching too. Oh well, I guess we won't need pictures to remind us of that wonderful occasion. It was the happiest time of my life and I'm sure I could never forget that!

I received a letter from Doug yesterday and was sure glad to hear from him after so long. Apparently Gerrie hasn't told him too much because he did write a very friendly letter. I hope she doesn't tell him a lot of false tales because I'd sure hate that to break up our friendship. We've always been very good friends and I want to keep it that way. Honey, have you seen or heard from Gerrie lately?

Darling, I neglected to do one thing while I was home. I forgot to file my income tax! We were told that because of being in Korea we would have six months to file after we got back. Now they tell us that it is only sixty days. That doesn't leave me much time and I had forgotten all about it. I can't get it taken care of here, and by the time I get to Colorado Springs the post office is closed. Honey, I'm sending the W-2 form. Do you think you could get it taken care of? I think all you need to do is take it to the post office. Tell them that I was in Korea and I'm sure they'll understand. I hope it doesn't inconvenience you too much honey. I'm terribly absent minded! I could just as well have had it taken care of when I was home.

Well darling, it's getting late again, so I'd better go to bed. Don't worry about me – I'm getting along alright. I hope everything is O.K. with you honey. Take it easy and don't work too hard. I'll bet those fish your dad caught are tasty. Eat one for me honey. Say hello to everyone. I'll write again soon.

Your ever-loving husband,

Sincerely, Med

P.S. The withholding statement is sure beat up. Hope they can read it.

June 9, 1952

Monday

Hello Darling,

 Well honey I didn't get a letter written over the weekend, so I thought I had better write a few lines tonight. Darling, my entire weekend was spent sightseeing. One of the fellows here and myself decided to get around a little for a change, so we went into Colorado Springs and rented a car. A 1951 Ford Convertible. Real nice huh?

 Honey, I was really surprised at the beautiful scenic attractions that Colorado has, and they are all so surprisingly close to Camp Carson. We visited the famous "Pikes Peak", "Garden of the Gods", "Cave of the Winds", "Will Rogers Shrine of the Sun", and other places. We made quite a trip of it. Honey, I don't know if you have ever seen these places or not, but they're extremely beautiful. Pikes Peak is 14,115 feet above sea level. Darling, you can just imagine the view you would get from there. All these places are situated in the mountaintops and nice roads all the way. At the tops of these resorts, they have nice, peaceful lodges. It's really quiet up there honey. What an ideal spot for a honeymoon! Darling, if I'd have known that it was so beautiful around here, we could have come up here for our honeymoon. You really must see them for yourself to appreciate their beauty.

Oh Lila, I was lost without you! I kept thinking to myself how wonderful it would have been if you were here. Darling, I can't enjoy anything without you. After I'm out of this mess, I'll want always to share such pleasures with you.

I can see now why Colorado Springs is such a tourist town. People come from all over the United States to see these places. Honestly honey, "Garden of the Gods" is just like being in paradise. It's the most beautiful picnic grounds I have ever seen. If you haven't seen it, I'd sure like you to sometime. It did cost a little for the rental of the car and all, but not too expensive. I just had to break the monotony some way! I would never have seen these places without a car.

Honey, I picked up a few souvenirs. I'm sending one to you right away. It isn't anything much, but darling, it says in words just how I feel for you, and I couldn't help buying it.

Darling, I received another of your wonderful letters today. I'm so happy when I get them. I'm certain that I couldn't last these months out if I didn't receive them!

Honey, I note what you said about the folks not hearing from me, and I'm really shocked because I wrote the last letter! I'm not saying this just to cover up anything, but I did! I'm sorry that they feel the way they do, but it isn't my fault if the letter doesn't get there. I've always been fairly regular about writing to them. I write more letters than all the rest of the guys in the barracks put together. I wrote Dick & Nellie a letter at the same time, so chances are they didn't get it either. Please tell them what the scoop is because I don't want them to think I've forgotten them completely. That really is the way it happened, honey. I wrote them both the first part of last week. I also haven't heard from either of them in quite some time, so they shouldn't talk. Just to keep peace in the family I'll write tonight. Will you give them the word? Honey, maybe you won't have to spank me when I get home, huh?

As yet I haven't been able to get a money order, but I will right away and send you some money. Seeing as how I was overpaid this month, I probably won't get any at all next month. If I don't I guess you'll have to send some back.

The weather here is getting hot and dry. How is it there?

Well darling, I've blabbed long enough. I'll close for now. Take it easy and be a good little wife. I'll write again soon.

Your Ever-loving Husband,

Med

P.S. Darling, I'll have to tell you again how much I love you – and how very much you mean to me. I could just picture you at my side during the weekend. I honestly won't be able to stand it longer than August.

June 16, 1952

My Dearest Wife,

Well honey, I didn't write over the weekend again, but I did have very good intentions. I didn't go anyplace but still I just couldn't seem to write. This probably sounds odd, honey – sometimes it's very difficult to concentrate. I imagine you know what I mean, and there really isn't much to write about. I say the same thing over and over each time I write. Do my letters bore you, honey?

Darling, I received another of your letters last Saturday. I'm always happy and relieved to hear from you. You write very sweet letters, honey, and they're regular about coming. That means everything!

Darling, I'm sorry that I forgot to give you any suggestions as to a Father's Day gift. I meant to last time I wrote but it just slipped my mind. I guess that isn't a very good excuse, is it? But honey I wouldn't have been much help anyway. I don't have any idea of what he needs or anything of the sort. Mom should know more about that than I do. I'll be glad when I get out so we can take care of these matters together. But darling, you have very good taste and I'm sure that whatever you decided on would be appreciated by anyone.

Honey, I'll bet that card table from your girlfriend is beautiful. I agree it was sure nice of her to send it. I guess I never met her, did I? Gee honey, I'll bet we sure have a lot of nice things now. I can hardly wait until I see them.

Well honey, I went to the doctor again today because my condition seemed to get worse over the weekend. It's very discouraging because it's coming back again as bad as it was at first. It doesn't look as though I will ever be cured! The doctor seemed to think that it could be my kidneys that are causing the infection. He said not to be alarmed but if there is anything wrong with them it may be serious, and I'd probably have to go to the hospital. I'll have an x-ray of them Wednesday, so until then I guess there isn't much to do but hope and pray that everything will be alright.

Lately honey I've had a sharp pain in my back and the lower portion of my body has become somewhat infected. So, I guess this trouble isn't quite as simple as I thought it was. Oh darling, I hope they can do me some good this time. It's very miserable, but most of all I want to be cured before I come home to you, if it's at all possible.

I want you to know all about it, honey, but please don't worry. I guess that's part of being married – to share each other's problems. I just don't want to have too many of them!

Darling, I'll let you know what the scoop is as soon as I have the x-ray. I also found out another thing. If this trouble isn't cleared up before the 27th of August I probably won't get out, because anything that develops after coming in the Army must be cured before I get out. Darling let's hope and pray that it will be. I couldn't stand it if I had to stay any longer!

I hope everything is going alright for you, honey. Please take it easy and don't overwork. I'll write again soon, so until then.

Loving and missing you Always,

Your Husband,

Med

P.S. I'm glad you liked the surprise. It was really very simple, but the verse itself said just what I feel for you.

June 19, 1952

Hello Dearest,

Well darling, how's everything going? Fine, I hope! Honey, I've been thinking about you all day – more than usual – and wishing how I could be with you. If only I could only come home, even if it were just a short time, I'd feel so much better. But then I guess I'd pay the penalty when I got back. You know what I mean!

Honey, it's been a long time now since I left and still, I'm not cured by any means. Darling, I'm going to feel badly if this condition isn't cleared up by the time I get out. If it isn't by then, chances are it never will be. Yesterday I spent the entire morning in the hospital having x-rays taken of my kidneys. The doctor seems to think they could be the cause of the trouble, but I hope he's wrong. A kidney ailment is something I've always dreaded. Anyway honey, tomorrow I'll go back to the hospital and find out what the scoop is. By then the x-rays will be developed. I'll write and tell you all about it honey, so don't worry.

Thanks, honey, for taking care of Father's Day for us. Dad always did like nice shirts, and I'm sure he would appreciate anything from you. He has remarked several times in his letters how much he thinks of you and how glad he is that I married you. They both feel the same about you and I'm glad for that! Darling, I think you're pretty swell myself. I only wish that I could see you now and tell you exactly what I mean.

Sixty-nine more days to go, huh? It's getting shorter, but how awfully slow! I'm afraid August will be the slowest month of all, but also the last one. That's what counts!!

Honey, I don't blame you for being tickled about the raise. $10.00 is always a big help. I guess they're beginning to realize that Med's wife is quite a little wheel and should have more money, huh?

Darling, you mentioned that you got another of the $50 checks that was taken out before we were married. Evidently that was for the month of May because your allotment checks won't begin until June, even though you probably won't receive one until the latter part of

July. Honey, be sure and tell me when you do receive one because if by chance you don't, I can go to the finance section here and find out why you're not getting them. This happens sometimes. Yes honey, I'm glad you put the check in the bank. We'll need all we can get.

Darling, it sounds like you're really getting a lot of nice gifts. I agree, we are getting a pretty fair start. I can hardly wait to see everything.

Well honey, it's late once again, so I'd better close for now. Take it easy and say hello to everyone for me.

With the deepest of love,
Your Lucky Husband,
Med

P.S. Have you seen Dick or Nellie lately? They haven't answered my last letter which was written over two weeks ago. I can't understand why they don't write!

June 22, 1952

Sunday

Well honey, I wasn't going to write tonight because I haven't felt good all day, but I'll scribble out a few lines anyway.

Darling, I received another of your letters yesterday. I'm always contented and happy when I hear from you. Honey, it's sweet of you to be so concerned about me, but please don't worry too much about my trouble. However, I guess it's only natural. I know I'd feel the same if anything were wrong with you.

    I went back to the doctor Friday. He didn't say too much about the x-rays. The damn place was so crowded with boneheads standing around trying to get their ears full that he (doctor) didn't get a chance to tell me much. However, he did say that there weren't any stones in my kidneys and that was the main thing he was looking for. He did say that my left kidney didn't show up as plain as the right one. He asked if I'd had any pain to speak of in the left side and I told him no. That's all he said, which isn't very much. I still think something is wrong because he kept asking me if I've had any pain in the left side of my back. He told me to come and see him again tomorrow, so maybe he'll be able to tell me more.

    Darling, you seemed worried so that's why I'm writing a few lines tonight. Please don't worry anymore, honey, because I think I'll be O.K. Perhaps – in time- I'll get over this damn stuff! I'd hate to think I'll be this way for the rest of my life!

    Honey, I'll tell you more when I talk to the doctor again. This is just a note tonight, honey, but I feel kinda sick, so think I'd better go to bed. I'll write again soon. Be good honey and take good care of yourself!

With All My Love As Usual,

Your Husband, Med

July 1, 1952

My Darling Wife,

    Honey, I received another of your wonderful letters today. I'm always so happy to hear from you. Honey, you say the sweetest things to me, and believe me, I sure like to hear them! I just wish that I were home now so I could hear them from you in person.

    Darling, I too would like so very much to come home over the weekend, but I still don't know whether it would be wise. You know what I mean! Honey, I hate to keep using that as an excuse, but after all, it is true. Darling, believe me, that is the only reason why I haven't been home a long time ago. Several of the guys from Utah are going home for the 4th and I could easily get a ride with any of them. Honey, a day or two at the most is all I could stay, and then that leaving part would be much worse again. Darling, we've managed to tough it out this long, so we may as well wait until that wonderful day of August 27 rolls around. It really isn't too long now, is it?

    Honey, maybe I shouldn't have told the folks about my kidney trouble, but I did it for the simple reason that in case I did go to the hospital they would know beforehand. Darling, I feel much better again, so please don't worry, and tell mom not to worry. I'm O.K.! Whatever you want to tell them about it is O.K. with me, so don't worry about that.

I'm glad that Doug came to see mom, but I also wish that he and Gerrie would have come to see you too. I guess Gerrie has told him several things that probably aren't true. I wish she would grow up and act her age. I hate to think that this will come between Doug and me.

Honey, have you seen Jay and Mary lately? They haven't written either. I can't figure out what gets into people. I guess they're teed off at something too, but if that's the way people want to be I don't care either. I guess Jay has let his religion go to his head, huh?

Well honey I guess I've gossiped about enough. I'm out of paper so will close for now.

Take it easy honey, and don't work too hard. I'm thinking of you constantly darling, and wishing I could see you, but it won't be long now. Honey, I was paid yesterday so I'm sending more money.

With Deepest Love,

Med

July 8, 1952

Hello Dearest,

How's my sweet little wife today? I hope you're doing alright.

Honestly darling, I haven't quite come to my senses yet. It still seems as though I should be home with you.

Honey, as much as I tried to fight it, I still felt awfully lonely and depressed going back. Darling, it was so wonderful being with you – if only for a short time! Each time I come home and then leave again I realize just a little more how much you mean to me. Darling, you were so sweet and kind to me while I was home. Thank you for everything!

I wish that guy hadn't have come so soon because I did want to say so much to you. But honey, I'm sure you realize how I feel towards you. No one else could possibly ever take your place! Darling, if there were only more women on earth with dispositions like yours, I'm sure there would be many happier guys in the world. Lila, I love you very much and I'll do my best always to keep you happy.

Honey, maybe it was a good thing that we left early because we ran into the worst hailstorm I've ever been in in my life. It chipped the paint on the car. We were in a desolate section of Utah when it happened, so all we could do is park the car and wait for the storm to pass over, which took two hours. We finally reached Camp Carson at 3:30 the next morning, making it a 14-hour trip. Other than the storm everything went alright, so I hope you didn't worry too much honey. We drove careful.

Darling, I was surprised to see that you knew Jack Strong. He is a real nice kid and he also remarked how nice he thought you were. And darling, I certainly agree with him!

Honey, I received your ever faithful letter today, and I appreciate your writing that night. I was awfully anxious to hear from you.

Honey, my trouble doesn't seem to be bothering me yet. Let's just hope that it doesn't in the future. I don't care darling; it was worth it! And, if I get a chance I'll come home again. Darling, thank your dad again for everything. It was sure swell of him. I want to write the folks so will close for now. Say hello to everyone. I'll write again soon.

Your

Ever-loving Husband,

Med

July 11, 1952

My Darling Wife,

Well honey, I have some spare time today so now is as good a time as any to write. Honey, I should have written last night but I dropped off to sleep before I could get started. Darling, I'm always offering excuses but it's the best I can do.

I received two more letters from you in the past two days. Darling, I'm always pleased to hear how things are with you and that everything is O.K. I'm always concerned about you honey – more now than ever!

Darling, I was very relieved to hear that we're not going to be parents yet. Honey don't think that I'm dreading the fact because I'm not. If we were to have one now, I'd love it, of course, but we should wait for a few months yet. What do you think? But darling, it takes two and if you want one before too long, I'm sure we can arrange it. Ha!

Darling, I'm actually surprised about my condition. As yet, I haven't noticed a thing. And after all those sessions we had it should be acting up now if it's going to. Oh honey, I hope it doesn't. I'll be so happy the day I'm free from that mess. It really is miserable. In fact, I can't even act myself when it's that way. Let's keep our fingers crossed that I'm O.K., huh?

Honey, I also received the picture yesterday. It's sure nice. The bigger they are the better they look. I'll keep that picture always honey, as it reminds me of the most wonderful day of my life. But darling, there will be many more when we are together for keeps. Just 46 more days, huh?

Lila, it was sure wonderful talking to you on the phone that night. The connection was very clear. It seemed almost as though you were in the next booth. Darling, it does cost quite a little bit, but I'll call as often as possible.

As yet I don't know of anyone who is going home on the 24 th , but I'll keep inquiring. I'll keep trying darling, but don't expect me.

Honey, I hope that deal doesn't make you too sick. Please take it easy and don't work too hard. Honey, I worry about you also.

I'll bet it's nice to have your mother home again. Say hello to your folks for me. Honey, I want to mail this now, so I'll close.

With All My Love, Darling

Med

July 15, 1952

Hello Dearest,

Well honey, I slipped up again on my letter writing over the weekend, so thought I'd sneak in a few lines on government time. It's strictly against Army regulations but I want this letter to be in the mail this morning – regardless!

Darling don't think I don't want to write because I do, very much. Sometimes when I start a letter, I just can't think of a thing to say. They're all about the same thing over and over, so honey, don't get too bored. I'll try to do better in the future.

I received another of your ever faithful letters yesterday. Honey, you've sure been regular all these long months about writing to me. I appreciate it so much; I don't know what I would have done without them. Especially in Korea! Darling, you'd be surprised how your letters would snap me out of the mood I was in. I felt almost like fighting the war all by myself.

Darling, even though we didn't spend much time together before I went overseas, I could tell all along how much you really meant to me. And now that feeling grows stronger every day. I love you very much, Lila, and I'm so thankful that we were married. We haven't had much time together, but darling it won't be long now. How wonderful it will seem not to have to leave you and come back to a hole like this.

Darling, you mentioned how much fun you thought it would be to use all the nice gifts we have received. I certainly agree, honey. I'm getting more anxious every day to do so.

Honey, will you do me a favor? Look in the car ads and give me an idea of what a '49 Pontiac or Mercury would cost. Also, a '50 Chev. I just want to compare the prices there with the ones here.

Honey, remember the Pontiac I was telling you about? Well, it's been sold. A car like that always is. I also have spotted a nice looking '50 Chev for $1,545.00. It may be a little bit high so that's why I want you to quote some prices. I wouldn't buy one yet anyway, honey, not until I come home. But darling, I won't do anything without consulting you first. If you think we should wait until I come home, we sure can. The only reason I've even thought of buying a car here is because of bettering the price. Let me know what you think about it, honey.

I received another letter from Doug. He still seems to be friendly enough, so maybe Gerrie hasn't said too much. I sure hope she wises up. Doug said she is looking for a job there so maybe that will help.

Well honey, there isn't much more to say for now. I hope everything is going alright. Are you feeling O.K. now, honey? You'd better be! Say hello to your folks and Marilyn for me. I'm glad you two are going to shows honey. It does help break the monotony. I'm still feeling alright, so let's hope that I'm finally cured.

I'll close for now, darling.

With The Deepest of Love,

Your Husband, Med

---

16 July 1952

My Dearest Wife,

Well darling, I thought I'd write a few lines tonight because you probably won't be hearing from me for the next few days. I'm going to take a little trip!

Apparently, they don't have enough Military Police around here so they're letting some of the men sort of fill in for them. Especially the ones that aren't doing much – meaning me. I'm going with another fellow to Rapid City, South Dakota, to pick up a prisoner who has been A.W.O.L., and bring him back here. I've talked to other fellows who have had the same assignment, and they say it is a pretty good deal unless, of course, the prisoner gives you a lot of trouble. But we'll carry guns and handcuffs, so I don't think he'll try to get away. At least I'll get away from this hole for a while. Please don't worry honey, and I'll write to you as soon as I get back.

Darling, I received another letter from you yesterday. I'm glad to hear that you're feeling alright, and everything is O.K. back home. Honey, I know what you mean about a lot of fuss and confusion around the house. It used to be the same way at home. But I guess we should get used to it because we'll probably have a dozen kids of our own to tear up the house. Ha! Gee honey, I hope not!!

Oh Lila, I'm getting so homesick to see you that I'm almost ready to take off again and come home. Darling, it's wonderful just to be near you – and see you. I'm getting so tired of living like this that I could die! Honey, I love you so much – these next 41 days have got to go by fast. I couldn't take any more! Darling, it's been rough on both of us, but let's thank God that we're nearing the end instead of just starting.

Well dearest, this is going to be a short letter, but I did want to write to you before I left. We'll be leaving sometime tomorrow on the train. We'll travel first class of a Pullman, so that part of it should be nice.

Be good honey, and don't work too hard. Say hello to your family for me. Are you getting a tan yet? Remember – you said you were going to lay in the sun.

I'll close for now, darling.

With My Deepest of Love Your Husband,

Med

P.S. I saw the doctor today (just for a checkup) and he said as far as he could tell that I was cured.

22 July 1952

Hi Sweetheart,

    Well honey, I made it back from a long and boring trip, so thought I'd write a few lines today and let you know that everything went O.K. Honey, the reason I say boring is because we had to go on a bus. Isn't that some deal? There is only one train every two or three days in and out of Rapid City, so naturally we had to do the next best and take a bus. It was awfully inconvenient trying to handle a prisoner on a bus. He didn't give us any trouble, so that meant a lot. Darling, you can imagine how miserable and tiresome it would be traveling 1,000 miles (both ways) on a bus in this hot weather. I thought I'd die before we got back! And another thing; I don't care for South Dakota. Even though there is some beautiful scenery there, the cities aren't very modern and up to date – especially Rapid City! I'd sure hate to live there! Honey, I haven't been any place yet that compares with good old Salt Lake, and I don't think I ever will. I hope they don't ask me to go after anymore prisoners because once is enough.

    Darling, I received three more of your wonderful letters since I got back. You always write nice letters to me, but I think they're getting better. You cute little shit! I'd sure like to be there now and give you a big smooch – and something else! I love you very much honey and it's growing deeper and deeper. Darling, I'm so near and yet so far away from seeing you. These next 35 days are going to go by very slow – at least it seems that way to me. But we should be thankful that it's nearing an end.

Thanks for the check darling, it was certainly sweet of you to send it. I'm glad that it wasn't one of those $50 ones. I guess I didn't really need it, but money always comes in handy, huh?

Yes honey, it was nice of Mrs. James to give us the beautiful vase. I guess she doesn't agree with the rest of the neighbors around there, that I'm a no-good. But then that works both ways. I think they're fanatical fools!

Thanks for sending the list of cars honey. There really doesn't seem to be much a difference in price with the ones in Denver, but I'm almost sure that the Denver cars are in better condition. Some of them are just like new. I'll keep watching, darling. There isn't any sense in buying one until I'm ready to leave here anyway.

Honey, you asked if I would like to have you here as a bed partner. Oh, you little bugger! Darling, if I soon don't have you, I know I'll go crazy! It was wonderful last time honey, and it will get better as time goes on.

Yes honey, I'll eat your fruit. I'll bet you really did a good job canning and I'm glad my little wife is on the ball and looking ahead.

Honey, I'm going to be busy tomorrow, so when you call the folks next time will you tell them that I made it back alright? I'll write to them soon.

I'm going to a show with Jack Strong tonight. He

is really a nice kid – and he still tells me how much he liked you. You're well thought of honey, and I certainly agree with people. I'm happy to have you as my wife.

It's hotter here than it has been so far. I'll be glad to get out of here. Don't work too hard honey and say hello to everyone. I'll write again soon.

With All my Love,

Med

July 27, 1952

Hello Dearest,

I've been worrying about you all week, so I thought I'd feel better if I wrote a few lines today. Darling, the reason I'm worrying is because I haven't heard from you in almost a week. Honey, I know it just isn't you to wait that long. There must be something wrong with the mail – perhaps. Nevertheless, I hope everything is alright with you and your family. It's easy to let your imagination run away with you, isn't it? I know how you must feel when the letters don't come as often as they should. Honey, like I've always told you – you've been very sweet and faithful about writing to me. Wish I could have done as well. I do hope the letters get through tomorrow, I'm awfully anxious to hear from you.

Darling, I haven't done a very good job of writing this past week myself. They've organized a ball team here and I'm on it, so that explains how I've spent most of my free time lately. We have done well in our last few games and if we do happen to win the tournament, we will take a trip back east. Indiana, I think, and play for the championship. Good deal, huh? This will probably happen after I'm discharged, but I hope it doesn't. It could be a nice trip for all of us.

Darling there really isn't much to talk about. Everything is about the same around here, just as dull and monotonous as ever. The time is dragging by awfully slow – more so than ever. One whole long month to go! I hope it will soon pass. I'm almost crazy. No matter where I go or what I do I still have that same old feeling of loneliness and discontentment. Honey, when I go into town and see other guys walking around with their wives or girls, I can't hardly stand it. Darling, it was so wonderful having you with me wherever I went and being able to call you my own. Oh honey, it's been so terribly miserable being like this all summer. That's why I say that if it were going to be much longer, I couldn't stand it! I'm very serious honey. I didn't realize before that it was such a mental strain. You know very well how I feel; it's been rough on both of us. It just can't happen ever again!

Well honey, I'm running out of paper. I'll close for now. Take care of yourself and write soon.

With All my Love – As Ever,

Your Husband –

Med

August 13, 1952

My Dearest Wife,

Well darling I hope you haven't been worrying too much because I made it back safe and sound and on time. I really do enjoy traveling by air even if it is expensive. The plane was air- conditioned – almost chilly and that was really appreciated by me. Honey, I wanted to write last night but I was so sleepy that I just couldn't. I hope you understand.

Darling, believe me when I say I love you more every time I see you. Honey, I always did, but it's getting to a point where I can't stand being away from you. I hope you don't think I'm a big bawl-baby but saying goodbye to you is getting to be almost unbearable. Darling, when this is all over, I never want to be without you again. You're so much a part of me that's it's like losing an arm every time we are separated. Oh honey, I love you more than words can express! You're my whole life. Please don't ever let anything happen to you. I want you always, darling, just the way you are.

Lila, I've been worrying about your back. Please go to the doctor, won't you? I hope it's nothing serious and be sure to tell me all about it.

Darling, we only have a short time left, but I feel worse than ever before. I didn't think I could love any girl as much as I love you. Oh honey, I couldn't leave you again. I'd rather die first!

As far as I know everything is the same here. I mean I'll still be getting out the 27th. It's only thirteen days now, but each day will seem like a week. I'll be so proud and happy the day we can move into our own apartment. I'm so thankful that you're my wife and I'll try my best to please you – believe me!

How's your job going now? I hope they didn't get too mad at you for being late so much. Honey, if they are you just tell them that they're lucky I didn't keep you away longer. If we had it to do over again, I would have.

Darling, how is the car running? I'm sorry that I left you with so many things to do, but it won't be long now and I can take care of them myself. Honey, if you must lose some work again to get the insurance taken care of, please let it go and I'll do it as soon as I get home. It's really my job anyway.

Have you noticed the car leaking oil? I don't think it's too serious, but it won't do any harm to watch it for a while. When you write honey, please tell me all about it.

Oh darling, I can't stop telling you how much I love you. It's a wonderful feeling and I'm glad it happened to me. You're so sweet and wonderful. How happy I am that I am lucky enough to be your husband. I don't know how I'm going to stand it before I see you again. The time is dragging so slow; I knew it would. But the thought of just coming home to you for the last time – excites me.

Well darling, I can't think of much more to say for

this time. I'm going to try and write the folks tonight also, but you could call them anyway, huh? Darling, did you pick up my navy-blue suit? Take real good care of yourself honey. Say hello to everyone for me. I'll write again soon.

With Deepest of Love,

Med

August 15, 1952

Hello Darlin,

How's everything going honey? I hope you're getting along alright and not having any trouble with the car.

Darling, I received your ever welcome letter yesterday and was so thrilled and relieved to hear from you. Oh honey, I'm missing you more now than I ever have. I've always loved you, but this last time home seems to have made more of an impression than ever before. Darling, I love you so much that I can hardly sleep at night. You're the sweetest little wife on earth and I'm thankful that I was lucky enough to marry you. I hope I can live up to the things you'll expect of me. I'll try honey, honest I will!

Darling, the time is slowly slipping away. Just eleven more days and I'll be coming home to you for the last time. We hope! Oh Lila, if I ever must leave you again, I'm sure my heart would break. I can't think of anything that would be worse.

Maybe we should have a dependent or two, which might prevent my being called back in, what do you think? Honey, have you had your deal yet? I've also been wondering about that. Please let me know when you do.

Honey, have you been reading that book yet? It really might help to read it. I'm going to read it all when I get home because I'm not very smart when it comes to those things either. I think we should study up on the positions, don't you?

Honey, if and when you get the radio fixed in the car be sure to watch that it charges (amp meter) because we don't want that trouble again. It could easily cause a fire in the car somewhere. If it does happen again honey, but sure and have it taken care of – only don't take it to Streators!

Well darling, there isn't much more I can say for now. Oh, thank your dad for letting us use his garage. It's certainly nice of him.

I hope you're feeling O.K. honey. Be sure to see the doctor, won't you? Tell me all about it when you write again. I'll close for now.

With All my Love as Always Your Husband,

Med

The Final Chapter Camp Carson, Colorado

17 August 1952

My Darling Wife,

How's my sweet little wife feeling today? I hope you're alright honey, and everything is okay at home. I've been wondering and worrying about your back. I sure hope you've been to see the doctor. You'd better say yes!

Darling, I received another letter yesterday and I was as happy and thrilled as always to hear from you. Honey, believe it or not but your letters mean more to me now than they did when I was overseas. But I guess they should, after all, you are my wife now! Darling, I love every little thing about you. I'm so lost and alone that I hardly know which way to turn. I've counted and recounted the days, but they just aren't going by fast enough. Oh honey, I'll be so happy when a week from Wednesday gets here. According to the latest report, I'll get out between 10:00 and 11:00 on the morning of the 27th, so that should give me a pretty good start, huh?

I'm missing you darling, probably more than you realize. But it's a wonderful feeling knowing that I have such a sweet little wife waiting for my return. Honey, I never want to leave you again – never!

Darling, you told me about getting such a scare the other day and I don't blame you for being upset. Honey, why did the doctor say you couldn't give any blood? Maybe my imagination is running wild, but I'm under the impression that you're going to have a baby. You haven't mentioned in either letter anything about having your deal yet, so that's why I'm asking. Darling, please tell me if you are - I'd rather know now. It's true we didn't want one yet but if it's happened there's nothing we can do. Darling don't get me wrong because I'll be proud and happy, and I'll love it more than anything just knowing you're it's mother. But still honey, I'd like to know so please tell me. We've been lucky so far, but luck can't last forever.

I'm glad your dad got you a seat cover for the car. And honey, you're right, you won't get spanked now. Lucky girl huh? But maybe I can find another reason sometime. I'll keep watching.

Darling, you know I mentioned something about an oil leak before I left? Well, the more I think about it the more I think Streator's left some bolts loose when they worked on it. I can fix them when I get home, but honey, please watch the oil and don't let it get too low. That would ruin the motor in a very short time. Also, the power-glide oil. I know you'll do all this, but I'm just not myself if I can't worry about something. I guess I take after my mom, huh? Honey, if I remind you too much just tell me to wise up, will you?

Yes, honey it's been awfully hot here lately. I'll be glad to get out of this hole.

Well darling, there isn't much more to say for now. I hope everything is okay. How is your work going honey?

Please don't overdo yourself and get too tired. After all, the bank isn't the only place to work.

I'll close for now honey. Say hello to everyone for me. How is mom feeling now?

With All my Love, Your Husband –

Med

August 19, 1952

Hello Dearest,

Well darling, I'm awfully lonesome tonight so I thought I'd write a few lines. Maybe it will help huh? I don't know what I'm going to say though, each letter is only a repetition of the last one but honey, I hope you'll read it anyway.

I received your last letter yesterday and honey, I'll have to tell you how much I enjoyed reading it. Darling you ought to be spanked for always telling me that you can't write letters. They're wonderful honey, and I believe they're getting better each time. You say some of the sweetest things to me. I hope you'll always say them. Believe me, I'll try not to ever give you a reason which would change your opinion. I too think you're plenty wonderful yourself, darling, and I've loved and missed you more this last time than ever before. Oh Lila, I'm so lost and alone; I just don't care for anything except to come home to you.

Darling, you've touched the spot in my heart that I didn't think could ever be reached by any person. Lately I've thought over and over to myself how fortunate I was to meet and marry a girl like you. I've always loved you, but I guess being married to you has sort of grown on me because there's a feeling inside me now that wasn't there before. It's so wonderful having a companion – one you love and admire – and darling, I want it to be that way always. I couldn't stand it if I ever lost you!

Just think honey, if it hadn't been for Gerrie I'd probably never have met you. So, I guess I do owe her something after all. I hope she doesn't feel too badly towards us because I'm willing to forget all about it just knowing that she's the person who introduced me to you. I'm very grateful!

Darling, just think! Only one week from tomorrow morning and I'll be coming home. Isn't that wonderful? Honey, if they ever come after me again, please don't let them take me, will you? Maybe between the two of us we can throw them off. It's worth a try anyway, huh?

Honey, you mentioned that the bank didn't dock you a cent for all the time you missed (my fault). I don't blame you for feeling good about it. It's certainly nice of them. I hope they'll always do that when I keep you home. Ha!

Darling, suit yourself about getting an apartment now. I think it would be a good deal if you can find too, having such a wonderful little wife and being separated from her is almost more than a man can stand.

Oh Lila, I love you so much. I'm so lost without you that I just don't care for anything here or anything that goes on around me. My every thought is back home with you. Honey, you once mentioned that it would be awful to love a person so much and then not be married to one another. I just couldn't stand it if we weren't married. I'm so happy that it worked out the way it did – I'll always be happy!

Honey, I received a letter from you yesterday and one today. I appreciate them so much, honey: they're sweet and always cheer me up. I wish that I could receive three or four a day from you. That's how much they mean to me, honey. I'm not complaining, you've always been very faithful about writing to me. It's just that I love you so much, and a letter always brings us so much closer. I'd be lost without them honey, believe me!

I'm glad that your back is feeling much better again. I hope that it will continue to do so. Please do as the doctor tells you, won't you honey? I was beginning to think that it was something serious.

Darling, in a way, I'm glad we're not having a baby yet. It will mean a great deal to us if we can hold off for a while, but I'm getting kind of anxious and excited myself. When it does happen though, I'll be as happy as you will. I think! And it's true that it would help to prevent me from coming back in the Army. But there's still plenty of time. We'll talk about it some more when I get home, okay?

Honey, you asked if I had any plans as to how I was coming home. I don't know yet. That fellow with the Buick that Jack and I came home with on the 4 th of July is getting out the same day, so we're going to ask him tomorrow if he is loaded yet. If he isn't I think that would be a good deal, don't you? Anyway, I'll decide within the next few days and let you know. Flying would be nice but it is also expensive.

Darling, you asked me if my kidneys or other condition had been bothering me. No, it hasn't bothered me at all since I got back, and I'm sure glad about it. So apparently, I'm cured, huh? I certainly, hope so because it really was miserable and sometimes quite painful.

I'm glad you got insurance on the car, and it really sounds like a good deal to me. Now when I wreck it – it won't be a total loss anyway, huh?

Honey, have you had the radio fixed yet? You hadn't mentioned it so that's why I was wondering. If you do, watch the amp meter and see that it doesn't discharge like it did before.

I received a letter from the folks today. I'm glad to hear that mom is feeling better. Darling, it's only five more days now, so I don't see much need in writing to them again. I honestly can't think of anything to say now to anyone but you. Honey, maybe you could tell them that everything is O.K. from time to time. They'll understand and it'll only be a few more days now before I'm home.

I'm glad that you and Marilyn went to the show. It does help honey, I know! Say hello to Marilyn for me. I was going to a show with Jack tonight but found out I'm completely broke except for two cents, and so is he! Isn't that some deal? Oh well, it won't be long now anyway.

We're having a terrible rainstorm tonight. I hope it isn't that way in Salt Lake because I want it to be nice when I get home.

Well darling, I hope I haven't bored you with all this jibber-jabber. I enjoy writing to you honey, even though I repeat myself.

I hope everything is alright and you're not working too hard. Say hello to you folks for me. Good-night, sweetheart. I'll write again soon!

With the Deepest of Love,

Med

August 24, 1952

Sunday

Hello Darling,

Well honey, I guess this will be the last letter because I'll probably beat the next one home. And darling, there really isn't much to say anyway.

I received another of your ever-faithful letters yesterday. Honey, I always feel so much better when I hear from you. You do write well, darling, and I can't begin to tell you how very much your letters have meant to me during this long old grind in the Army. They're all in the world that have helped me through sometimes when I've been so discouraged.

But soon, darling, I'll have you to help me in person and not just in letters. Lila, you're the best thing that ever happened to me; I do need you so much! You've certainly helped me out of a rut. I doubt if I would have ever married anyone if I hadn't met you. Believe me, honey, I just didn't care! Darling, I'll tell you again how thankful I am that it turned out the way it did. I don't think we'll ever be sorry; I'll do my best to see that we're not.

Honey, I certainly do think that apartment is a good deal. From the way you described it, it really sounds modern and clean, and the price is the best thing yet. I had my doubts as to whether we would find anything that reasonable. Yes honey, I think I know where the Arlington Apartments are on 1st Avenue, and it suits me fine. You're sure on the ball honey. I don't think I could have done as well. We'll decide where we're going to stay when I get home, huh? I mean until the 1st of September.

Darling, thanks for the $10. I really didn't need that much but it will come in handy. You're sure a sweet little bugger, honey. I could eat you up!

Darling, I'm going to call you either Monday or Tuesday night, so there isn't any need in wasting all the space to tell you how I'm coming home. I'll tell you everything then. I think I will have called you before this letter gets there anyway.

Only three more days, honey, so that isn't so bad huh? I can hardly wait!

There isn't much more to say for now, so I'll be closing, darling. I'm glad you're feeling better, and everything is O.K. Don't worry about me – I'm alright. Tell the folks not to worry either. I'll see you soon, honey.

With All my Love to you Darling –

Med

Well, darling, I hop[e]
this letter will find [you]
in better spirits than
myself.

Honey, talking to
you on the phone las[t]
night meant everyth[ing]
in the world to me
but when I had to [say]
good-bye and hang u[p]
well, that was almos[t]
more than I could sta[nd.]
Oh, Lila, I love and m[iss]
you so much that I'm
almost out of my min[d.]
It just doesn't seem fa[ir]
that we should have
to be separated. I jus[t]

EPILOGUE

As I read each one of these letters, I could feel my father's emotions: sorrow, fear, excitement, doubt, and, most of all, his extreme love for my mother and his gratitude of being spared to come home and start a new life with the woman he loved. But life doesn't always play out the way that we plan, or even hope. Unexpected junctions mark each of our lives.

After he was honorably discharged from the U.S. Army, my father came back to Salt Lake City to his beautiful new wife. After honeymooning in Yellowstone National Park they returned, excited to cohabit their first apartment and begin their new lives together. It was during that time that life switched the tracks beneath them. My father became extremely ill and was taken to St. Mark's Hospital in North Salt Lake. There it was confirmed that he had polio. He spent an entire year in a hospital bed confined to an iron lung, not knowing whether he would die and, if he lived, how handicapped the horrible disease would leave him.

I wish I would have paid more attention when my dad spoke of his memories of the war or his time spent in the hospital, which was rare. I do remember him telling me when I was older that he recalled an "out of body" experience one day where his spirit was hovering over the door in the corner of the room as a team of doctors and nurses frantically worked on him to bring him back to life.

He also spoke of lying in the bed day after day and every single night, after my mom got off work at the bank, he could hear her high heels as she walked down the long corridor lovingly approaching his room. Her ever-faithful letters while he was in the Army and her heartbreaking, yet dutiful hospital visits never ceased. She stood up to each challenge without complaining and carried herself with dignity and full of grace. My mother was lovingly (and appropriately) nicknamed by her father, his "little peachy." She truly was as beautiful and sweet as a freshly picked summer peach. I never heard any type of harsh words or self-pity from her. She approached each day with a smile on her face, a kind word and an endearing wink, gifts she shared freely with everyone she met. When I think back on how she could have lived her life with resentment, I strive to remember her as my example of pure love, patience, kindness and a true faith in God.

It took years of rehabilitation for my father to be strong enough to find employment. There were no laws nor special interest groups then that looked out for those with handicaps. The polio ravaged his strong, athletic body making his muscles weakened and left him needing to wear a special leg brace on his left leg from hip to foot. He was classified by the U.S. Government and Army as 100% disabled but never qualified or received any sort of assistance. When strong enough, he enrolled at Steven's Heneger Business College and graduated with the anticipation of finding a job. He immediately found out what discrimination felt like. No one wanted to employ someone who wasn't "normal" by their standards. In even the darkest of times there are angels amongst us. Maurice Warshaw, who was founder of a very successful line of grocery/drug stores called Grand Central, hired dad to be part of his payroll department in the corporate office. Mr. Warshaw's own son Keith was stricken with polio, so he took a special interest in helping those who were struggling after this disabling disease. Dad remained a faithful employee there until the mid 1980's.

I was born August 19, 1955, three years after dad returned from Korea. My mom and dad wanted to have another child but were unable. One vivid memory I have, was the day my kindergarten class went to Utah's Hogle Zoo for our end of year field trip. After an exciting morning experiencing the wonder of all the different animals through the eyes of a 5-year-old, we were all seated together at the picnic tables to eat our "sack lunches". That's when I looked up and coming down the hill through the shade of the trees was my beautiful mother carrying my new baby brother, and my dad walking alongside them using his wood crutches. I ran to them with joy. They had just signed the adoption papers making Todd "legally ours" and they wanted me to be with them to share in this. We left together as a family. I was so happy and proud that I finally had a new baby brother to share my childhood with and, later, the rest of my life. I love my brother dearly and am closer to him now than I've been my entire life.

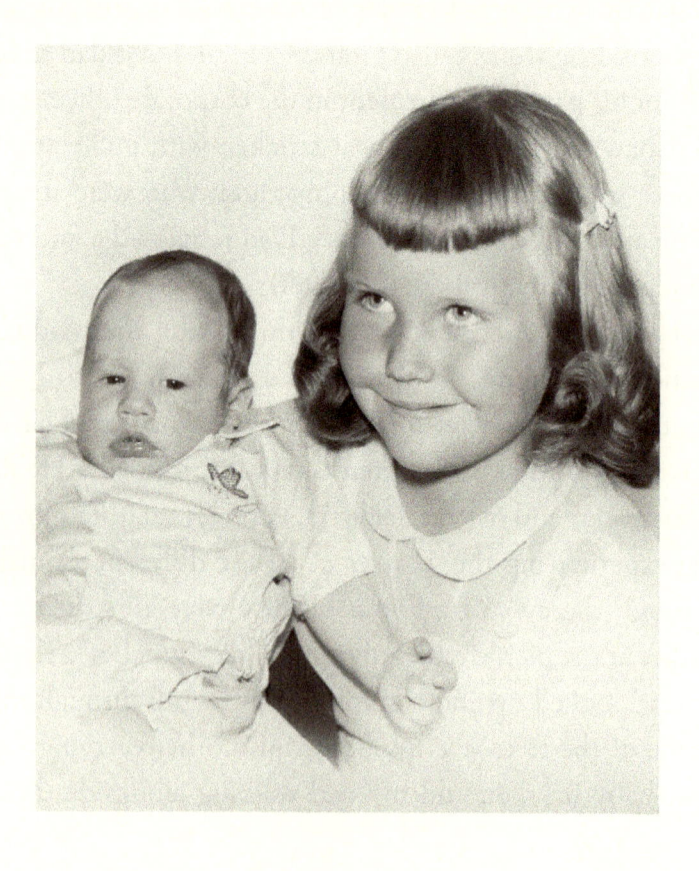

We had a good childhood enriched with loving grandparents, aunts and uncles and lots of cousins. Even though money was scarce, mom and dad managed to provide us with wonderful memories of family vacations, summer camp, camping in our little trailer and other extracurricular activities. Dad took Todd fishing and to ball games. I was privileged to be my mom's best friend, which I will forever hold dear to my heart.

My mother died at the young age of 62 years old, after a nine-month battle with lung cancer. It was one of the darkest days of my life. Although she suffered horrifically, she still managed to smile at me.

Throughout our lifetime dad drank. Popov Vodka. Mom covered it up well enough that few people had any idea. Out of respect to mom we kept it quiet. There were so many times that I wanted to lash out at my father for his meanness and anger towards us when he had been drinking, but I rarely did, both out of fear of my father and respect for my mother.

After mom died, dad's drinking became worse. He became angrier, more negative and miserable from the ongoing effects polio had on his crippled body. It was difficult to be around him, but out of consideration to mom we made sure he was taken care of. At 63 years old he became a full-time resident in a care facility. The house that my mother and father spent their lifetimes working to pay for, was turned over to the care center to pay for his residency. After just four years of living there in a private room we received notification that all the proceeds from his house had been exhausted and he would need to be put in a semi-private "veterans" room. It was at this point his dignity was gone. Due to his excessive drinking, he already had liver cirrhosis, a condition which we had expected him to die from years before mom. Broken, he found someone to bring him Everclear, which caused alcohol poisoning. I was notified shortly after he had slipped into a coma. He did not want the hospital notifying me or my brother while he was still conscious. On August 3, 1996, my husband, our children and I were with him as he took his last breath. Todd was living in Minnesota and did not have time to arrive.

It was nearly three decades after my mother's passing that I found the strength to go through the cedar chest that I had moved with me three different times. When I uncovered the box, I had no idea what contents it held. I know now that finding these forgotten letters was something meant for me. My father truly loved my mother, and, through whatever difficulties, she loved him back, until the end of her life.

Thank you, Mom and Dad. I will forever be grateful for your love and sacrifices. What you taught me, even painfully, has made me the person I am today. Dad was always quick to point out that I couldn't do something, or I couldn't have something. I now thank him for that, because it made me that much more determined that I could, I would and I did, many times over.

These precious letters were a gift of healing for me, one that surpasses my own understanding. My hope is that others reading your story may learn, as I have, that everyone is a library, and all too often we only take the time to read a few of their books. But often, somewhere in those bound covers, we can find understanding. And with it, forgiveness.

Love,
Kathy

There is no chance, no destiny, no fate,
that can circumvent, or hinder or control
the firm resolve of a determined soul.

— ELLA WHEELER WILCOX

Korean War Ended 32 Years Ago Today

WASHINGTON (AP) — It was called "the wrong war, in the wrong place, at the wrong time, and with the wrong enemy," and it took the lives of 54,259 Americans.

Saturday is the 32nd anniversary of the end of the Korean War and the U.S. Postal Service is commemorating that event by issuing a 22-cent stamp honoring "Veterans Korea."

"Our debt to Korean War veterans can never be fully repaid." Postmaster General Paul N. Carlin said Friday at a dedication ceremony attended by James Van Fleet, who commanded the United States 8th Army in the three-year war.

"We hope in this small measure to say 'thank you' both to the 5.7 million Americans who put their lives at risk, and especially to the more than 50,000 who gave their lives," Carlin said.

He mentioned that some Americans regarded gains in Korea as not worth the toll and recalled that Gen. Omar Bradley, then chairman of the joint chiefs of staff, called it "the wrong war, in the wrong place, at the wrong time, and with the wrong enemy."

The stamp, based on a photograph taken in 1950 by David Douglas Duncan, shows tired troops trudging through a mountain pass on the march seaward from the Chosin Reservoir.

Korea, the "land of the morning calm," was occupied by the Japanese from 1910 to 1945. After World War II, the country was divided into north and south sections at the 38th parallel with the Soviets to supervise the surrender of the Japanese in the north and the United States in the south.

In 1950, when communist North Korea invaded the newly formed Republic of Korea, the United Nations Security Council demanded the fighting be halted. President Harry S. Truman approved the use of American forces to support the South Koreans and soon a United Nations command under Gen. Douglas MacArthur was fighting the communists.

A truce was signed and fighting ended on July 27, 1953.

ABOUT THE AUTHOR

KATHY POULSEN ROMERO

Kathy has been married to her high school sweetheart Mike for 50 years. She is the mother of four incredible children ~ Josh, Eliza, Zach and Sarah and grandmother to three beautiful granddaughters. She has had the privilege of wearing many hats in her life but none more important than the joys of family and friends. Life is good.

more of your very sweet letters today
was very happy as usual, to hear from
you. Honestly Lila, I can't begin to
you just how very much they mean to
am so thrilled and relieved that I
know how to act. and darling, if I
couldn't ever hear from you again I
sure that I would go crazy. That
sound a little funny, but it's the
truth as I'm just living for your
and they are all that keep me going

            Darling, as I informed you in my
last letter, we are back in North Korea
again, but haven't been doing much of
thing since our return here. The si-
on seems to be pretty much hand and
fully quiet. as to whats going on a
what might develope in the future
cannot say. One day we are told
war is almost over and then the
day they tell us to be on the alert
for a big push by the Chinese, wh
will mean another big battle. So
the Cease-Fire talks haven't accomplished a
d is very doubtful if they will. But
guess I shouldn't complain as long as
ent any worse here, than they are at the
No kidding Lila, I'm getting so l
that I hate to even move around. The p
few days I haven't done one thing,
leep and eat and I can truthfully say
would much rather be doing somethi
the time seems to drag by so slow
also, allows a person to do a lot of th

Milton Keynes UK
Ingram Content Group UK Ltd.
UKHW020011061124
450708UK00001B/91